THE FOUR CORNERS

Where your estate plan becomes a living legacy

SHARED DRIVE

Collaboration for High Performers

Table of Contents

  "We can do that?"
  Look inside, then outward
  Enter this book where you are now
  Get to know Naples
    A toast to success
    The original Four Corners
  The Four Corners Estate Plan
    Corner One: Foundational Planning
    Corner Two: Protection Planning
    Corner Three: Opportunity Planning
    Corner Four: Tax Planning
    Connecting the Corners

  Understand your will
  Create a Living Will and designate a Health Care Surrogate
  Designate, or be prepared to designate, an attorney-in-fact

About the Book

LIKE ALL GOOD ESTATE PLANS, *THE FOUR CORNERS* IS A COLLABO-ration. Brad Galbraith is the primary author and original architect of the Four Corners Estate Plan. Mike Kilbourn and Robert O'Dell are co-authors, each contributing to the core manuscript and especially to the sidebars that accompany each chapter.

About the Authors

BRAD GALBRAITH

Brad is an attorney with Hahn Loeser & Parks LLP. He is a recognized national expert in advanced estate planning, and speaks frequently on planning and business succession to both families and professionals. Brad is board certified in Wills, Trusts and Estates by the Florida Bar Association.

Brad began his professional career as a Certified Public Accountant. After switching to the practice of law and seeing the ineffectiveness and inefficiency of traditional planning methods, he endeavored to find a better way to assist his clients with estate, tax, and business planning. As an estate planning attorney, he developed a model designed to provide clients with comprehensive, personalized estate, tax, and business succession plans that withstand the test of time.

Brad is the co-author of an extensive continuing education program for CPAs which has been published and distributed nationally. That program, titled Estate Planning for CPAs, has also been presented to thousands of CPAs throughout the United States. Brad is the co-author of *The Florida Domicile Handbook, Second Edition*, a 197-page guide that simplifies the process of moving to Florida and becoming a permanent resident. In addition to *The Four Corners*, Brad recently authored two books for attorneys titled *Family Limited Partnership Agreements Line by Line* and *Family Limited Liability Operating Agreements Line by Line*. Brad can be reached at BGalbraith@hahnlaw.com

MIKE KILBOURN

Mike Kilbourn, CLU, ChFC, CCIM, AEP, MSFS, president of Kilbourn Associates, Naples, Florida, has over 30 years experience as a family wealth transfer planning specialist and holds over 20 professional designations.

Mike is also the founder and chairman of the Wealth Protection Network®, a national network of estate planning professionals who work in concert to create and manage comprehensive estate plans.

Mike is a frequent expert guest on national financial network programs and has contributed to and authored numerous books and articles on investment, estate, and financial planning topics.

In addition to co-authoring *The Four Corners*, Mike is the author (with Brad Galbraith) of *The Florida Domicile Handbook— Vital Information for New Florida Residents*. He is also the author of *Disinherit the IRS*.

Mike can be reached at mike@kilbournassociates.com

ROBERT O'DELL

Rob O'Dell, CFP®, is a principal with Wheaton Wealth Partners, a wealth advisory firm with offices in the Chicago area and in Naples, Florida.

Rob's 20+ years of experience have helped shape Wheaton Wealth Partners' Planning Process, which involves the discovery and clarity of goals to formulate a detailed wealth management plan that is unique to each client. Prior to co-founding Wheaton Wealth Partners, Rob developed the financial planning arm for

LVM Capital Management, Ltd. In the mid-'90s, he worked in planning strategies and administration for the nation's leading charitable planning firm.

Rob can be reached at rob@wheatonwealthpartners.com

Acknowledgments

THIS BOOK IS THE CULMINATION OF YEARS OF GOOD INTENTIONS to put on paper many of my out-of-the box ideas about estate planning. When I started this project, I wanted to write something different—something more meaningful to the reader than just another book that explains the "rules" of estate planning. If you find that this book accomplished my goal, the thanks should be given to Greg Perry. Greg not only worked with me to write the text, but he filtered through countless ideas and stories to highlight those that would educate and inspire the reader.

My parents also deserve credit. Both of them spent the bulk of their careers as educators and, genetically, I think I am predisposed to educating others. If this book educates without reading like a textbook, Les and Marge Galbraith are responsible.

Finally, my beautiful wife, Lissa, and our five wonderful children, Maxwell, Cameron, Benjamin, Tatiana, and Callie, played a role as well. Each of them is quick to remind me that the books I've written previously are boring except to my fellow lawyers, and that if I want my family to read more than the first page of this book, it better be different than the others.

Well, different it is. I hope you enjoy the read.

Brad Galbraith
December 2011

Introduction

I don't want to achieve immortality through my work;
I want to achieve immortality through not dying.

Woody Allen

IT'S UNFORTUNATE THAT THE LANGUAGE OF ESTATE PLANNING IS SO weighted down by death. There's the death tax, death planning, deceased parties...and if our own human mortality wasn't heavy enough, how about some *probate* and *incapacitation* to cast a pall over your last will and testament? Estate Planning 101: Death and Disempowerment. And we wonder why people procrastinate.

It's time to re-frame the conversation with *life* and *empowerment* at the center of a precise estate plan configuration. We call it the Four Corners and it's a map for families who want to stay on offense, not defense. The Four Corners helps families explore how an estate can cultivate, create, and inspire.

Some families simply navigate the complexities of wealth better than others. What they do with their money now, and how they plan for it passing to their heirs, is guided by principles that transcend conventional thinking. In our individual practices we have encountered and advised families who possess an innate understanding that wealth—often great wealth—is merely the raw material for an enduring and thriving legacy. These families understand that, just as they define their wealth, they can also define their legacy.

Are they more financially savvy than others? Sometimes, but even that knowledge is often an organic product of the choices they've made. They've *learned* how to be smart, in other words. Is their emotional intelligence higher than the norm? After all, wealth creates at least as much stress as it alleviates, right? It's true that these families *can* have high degrees of emotional intelligence, but the very question places too much emphasis on emotional responses. These families have discovered a way to keep their emotions focused on an enriching legacy, not merely riches.

"WE CAN DO THAT?"

It can be an eye-opening, even mind-expanding, experience when the full range of estate planning possibilities is revealed. Some clients even question our scruples with furrowed brows and an "is that really legal?" look, as if we were recommending an exotic offshore tax haven. There's nothing exotic about the strategies in this book, but they have come from another world, specifically the rarified world of the super-affluent.

For decades, the families who measure their wealth in hundreds of millions and even billions of dollars have been crafting their estate plans using these legal structures and financial instruments. Along the way, their attorneys and advisors were generating fortunes of their own to create, maintain, and supervise these plans. But here's the surprise: Almost nothing here is new and most of the guiding laws have been on the books for years. Credit the transparency of our time and the rapid dissemination of information for making these strategies more visible and more affordable to implement.

The lower end of our business, the so-called "document jockeys," want nothing to do with this kind of planning. The questions they'll ask you are as formatted as their documents' templates and your answers go straight to a cut-and-paste in-basket. When the documents print, they can be very handsome indeed, often leather bound and practically oozing legal integrity. "You're welcome and here's your invoice; please pay at the window as you exit." Too harsh? Read on and absorb how an elevated kind of planning generates opportunities for you and your heirs, then come back to this page and imagine a meeting with one of those guys. You'll see straight through their leather.

LOOK INSIDE, THEN OUTWARD

To one degree or another, all estate planning is forward looking. The process itself puts a generational telescope to your eye and says: "That's your legacy out there, take a look, tell us what you see, and we'll plan to it." The problem is, most people are either too polite or too proud to admit that they didn't see much of anything. So they'll speak in abstractions like, "I want my wealth to create some security" or ". . . allow opportunities that I didn't have." That's true of nearly every person and not particularly helpful. Estate plans built from abstractions can end up reading like a list—"do this and don't do that." To future generations, especially those two or three branches up the family tree, that plan can become a burden, or worse, a prison.

A legacy envisioned in abstract and imprecise language, or even overly precise and narrow terms, is not a failure of imagination on *your* part, but on *ours*. So much estate planning has clients looking for their legacy in the wrong place.

Authentic legacies aren't distant constellations that hover overhead in indistinct shapes. They begin inside you, rooted in your values and aspirations, and are crafted so that they can live across generations. Authentic legacies evolve as they are passed on from person to person and so should an estate plan.

ENTER THIS BOOK WHERE YOU ARE NOW

If you're reading this book, let's assume you do not have your estate plan completely crafted and up to date. In other words, let's assume you're normal. It's true that most of the new clients we see have a will, and many have an advanced directive or living will. Some have formed trusts to house assets, but even those clients know they have more to do, but haven't made it a priority.

This is where some advisors drag you through the horror stories they delight in telling—the millionaire who died without a will, the trusts that were never funded, and the documents that were never signed. If they could rap your knuckles with a ruler, they probably would. Not here. Scolding and scaring is exactly the wrong way to begin a conversation around what's important and what's possible.

There's a story in the Zen tradition that can comfort those of us who are busy living life and *not* planning an estate. Here you go: The devotee asks the Master "how to enter Zen" and the Master tells him to "quiet the mind and listen...listen...Do you hear the stream?" And after several long minutes, gradually quieting the chatter in his mind, the devotee does; water flows in a far-away stream that requires all his focus just to hold the sound. "Enter Zen there," says the Master. The devotee is delighted with his meditative breakthrough, and the world is alive and peaceful in an entirely new way. But the incessant chatter soon returns and, with some embarrassment in his voice, he asks a second question, "What if I had not heard the stream?" Without hesitation the Master replies, "Enter Zen there."

Substitute "estate planning" for "Zen" and you know how to use this book and even how to plan: Start where you are. Estate planning isn't like a Christmas morning or a surprise birthday— everything doesn't have to be in place when the kids charge in or the front door opens. Estate planning is not an emergency; it

xvi   The Four Corners

is an opportune time to reflect, explore, and act. Our mission is
to help you transform your actions here and now into a legacy
that generates opportunities and inspires greatness—that's the
stream. We'll help you hear it clearly.

GET TO KNOW NAPLES

Naples is about as far south and as far west as you can go on the
Florida peninsula. Head due east and you're in the Everglades.
Head south and you had better be in a boat. It's a wonderful
place to live, to work, to grow up, and to grow rich. And richer.

Like all of Florida, Naples is heavily populated by retirees.
"God's waiting room" someone once quipped about Florida.
Except in Naples, the chairs are original Charles Eames and the
magazines are this month's *Robb Report*. Naples has some of the
highest family income in the United States. Family income in
Naples averages about $174,000—well above the U.S. average of
$75,000. In Naples, 19 percent of the families have annual incomes
of $200,000 and above, while across the U.S. it's less than 5 percent.
But there's a better way to measure wealth than just income.

Woods & Poole Economics, Inc. is an independent,
Washington, D.C.- based firm that focuses exclusively on long-
term economic and demographic projections at the county
level. Their projections extend 25 years into the future on more
than 900 variables, from population mix to retail sales. Woods
and Poole data has earned a high degree of confidence in the
chamber of commerce community and is often used to both
entice and support business relocation. Among the many mun-
dane variables they catalog and predict, one stands out to us—
the Woods and Poole Wealth Index.

The Woods & Poole Wealth Index is a measure of relative personal per-capita income weighted by the source of
that income. It moves higher in places where residents derive a

relatively larger portion of their income from dividends, interest, and rent. More than the zeroes on a person's weekly paycheck, these sources of income correlate more directly with wealth. And according to the demographers at Woods and Poole, Naples is among the top tier. And yet there's another way to measure the wealth of Naples.

A toast to success

Throughout the early 2000s, a tart and robust bi-coastal feud was taking place. The Napa Valley Wine Auction had been the top-earning wine charity event since 1981. It's where celebrity chefs and Hollywood stars clinked goblets with the vineyard elite. Millions of dollars were raised every year for area charities. A single bottle of cabernet sauvignon once went for $500,000. In 2001 Naples set out to top it.

The Naples Winter Wine Festival is an annual charity wine auction that in ten spectacularly generous years has surpassed the Napa Valley event as the most successful charity wine auction in the world. In 2011, the Naples event brought in $12 million, nearly doubling the tally of their West coast rivals. In just 10 years, the Naples Winter Wine Festival has raised nearly $95 million for under-privileged and at-risk children. Napa has been dethroned and the rarified world of big dollar charity events sees Naples in a new way.

It's what we, and the hundreds of other financial advisors who have set up shop here, could have told them years ago: When it comes to private wealth in the U.S., Naples is nearly unsurpassed. Among cities its size, Naples has no peers.

The original Four Corners

The Four Corners is a very real place in Naples and in Naples' history. It's the site of Naples' first traffic light and where the first two paved roads in the city intersected—5th Avenue South and the Tamiami Trail. It was during the 1940s at the Four Corners

xviii   The Four Corners

where the vision began to take shape of what this Gulf Coast paradise might look like in the decades ahead.

On the northeast corner of the Four Corners sat Club 41, a restaurant and club—the hub of Naples' social scene. It must have been a lively place, at least during the cool weather months. We're not historians, but we do know what happens when forward-looking people get together to talk about the kinds of legacies they hope to create.

Naples is where we live and where we practice. It's also where we have learned the core principles of the Four Corners Estate Plan. It's at this intersection of family wealth and uncommon planning that we have pitched our professional tents. We've been enriched in the process—by what we've earned, certainly, but also by what we've *learned*.

THE FOUR CORNERS ESTATE PLAN

Think of the four components within the Four Corners plan as interlocking pieces in a puzzle. The puzzle isn't complete until all four pieces are in and, like all puzzles, there's no single piece that *must* come first. You build a puzzle as you find a fit for the pieces already connected and, as you do, the puzzle reveals what the puzzle lacks. So there's no right or wrong way to construct your Four Corners plan; there's only your way. That said, we have sequenced the Four Corners in this book to align with how our conversations with clients often proceed. Our job is to take the myriad of estate planning instruments piled up on the table and work with you to build a finished plan that reflects your values and gives them room to grow over the generations.

Corner One: Foundational Planning

In this chapter you'll find some fundamental protective and preemptive strategies. Good planning means you protect the ball, but you *don't* have to keep it locked in the basement.

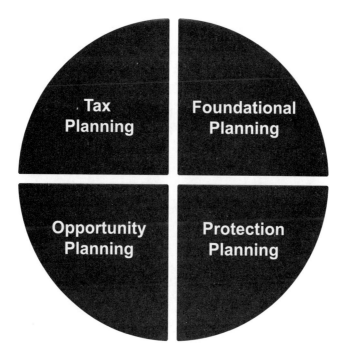

You should also understand that this isn't a primer or a text-book. We're not writing this for Dummies, Idiots, or chronic procrastinators. If you want advice on how to write a will, there are hundreds of helpful pages in the bookstore and on the web. In this book, we're taking you into territories that are more interesting and, yes, more challenging. We're going to explore what you value in life—what your internal values have generated in the outer world and how, after you've gone, they can continue to generate and support.

There are several components that absolutely must be a part of every plan, no matter how modest the estate or small the family. And in this chapter, we'll take you through them. It's not the longest chapter in the book, but it may be the most important.

Corner Two: Protection Planning

Protecting what's yours has a visceral quality to it: "There are threats and they must be kept out." That's true, but it's not enough. The Four Corners plan incorporates both traditional and non-traditional strategies for protecting your estate. Yet it's not about holding a purely defensive position. Protection in the Four Corners plan expresses a more nuanced understanding of real lives and how the generations interact with each other.

Protection is about understanding what's *possible:* the good, the bad, and the ugliness created by a big wall surrounding your house. There are more elegant ways—more effective, too—to keep the mongrels out. In this chapter, you'll discover them.

Corner Three: Opportunity Planning

This is where we most often hear the question: "We can do that?" And it's where we have the most interesting and enlightening conversations. That's because talking about opportunities is like an enthusiastic brainstorm session. Ideas start flowing. How about this? What if we...? Envisioning opportunities opens the door to a whole new way of thinking about a plan and inspiration fills the room. This chapter is about inspiration.

Corner Four: Tax Planning

For many people, estate planning is tax planning. It's about reducing the taxable value of your estate. Or as Mike Kilbourn put so perfectly in his book of the same name: Disinherit the IRS. Great idea. But tax reduction/avoidance is too often used like a chain saw when a better strategy—the Four Corners strategy—is to use a carving knife. That's because what works solely to reduce taxes might also sow the seeds of disharmony among the very people you thought you were helping. Four Corners planning creates a view of taxes broad enough to include the full range of possibilities and then invites you to make choices that balance everything (and everyone) that matters.

Four Corners estate planning is also about more than the estate tax. Gift taxes are in full view, so are income taxes and even the consequences of where you establish legal domicile. That makes this neighborhood in the Four Corners an important stop for every reader, even those with modest estate values that don't hit the estate tax mile marker.

Connecting the Corners

In the final chapter, we bring it all together with some practical guidance—street smarts, if you will. It's about how to build your estate planning team and what to expect from them. It's building collaborative relationships within your family and about how to talk about why your plan is what it is. The sad truth is, estate transitions are often fraught with difficulty. There are plenty of horror stories where decent planning still failed to form anything close to a legacy. Four Corners planning asks more from you but, then again, so does wealth. Our practices are platforms for helping wealthy families thrive for generations—financially and emotionally. If you ask our clients whether money makes their lives easier or harder, they'll usually say "both." There's emotional tension within wealth and it only gets tighter when the dollars move from one generation to the next. Understanding that tension, and relieving it, is at the core of the Four Corners. Let's go there.

Corner 1
Foundational Planning

My interest is in the future because I'm going to spend the rest of my life there.

Charles Kettering

W E'VE ALL SEEN A RELAY RACE. WHEN THE RUNNERS EXCHANGE THE baton, it's an elegant feat of anticipation and communication—beautiful in its own way, but *not* what we'll remember and talk about later. The relays we'll remember—the ones that are played again and again in TV highlights and personal memories—are when the baton is dropped. Heartbreaking to witness; excruciating to endure.

Now imagine that the runner approaching the exchange is one generation and the runner waiting to take the baton is the next. That baton represents the first generation's wealth and, you guessed it, it's dropped in the exchange.

Countless planning conversations have begun with different versions of that story. The details vary, but the ending doesn't: "I absolutely don't want that to happen." No one does. That's why the first order of business with a plan, and in this book, is to make sure nothing gets dropped, because it's impossible to pass wealth if the money is gone. Heartbreaking to witness; excruciating to endure.

This isn't the most interesting chapter in the book and it's certainly the shortest, but it could also be the most important. Run through the list below of must-haves and make-sures. All good? Excellent, we'll meet you at Corner Two. If not, stop kicking yourself and start moving. These few steps can keep the baton in your hands.

UNDERSTAND YOUR WILL

If you've done little or no estate planning, then drafting a will is Job #1. Most people think that, without a will, assets automatically pass to the surviving spouse. Not true, at least not in some states, including Florida, where the assets are divided amongst your spouse *and* your children. In fact, some of the most important things to understand about a will are what it *can't* do:

Wills don't help when you're disabled.
A will is effective only after you've finished the race and left the track. On the way there, it's likely that disability will color the last few laps. That means your will should be accompanied by the tools in the next section.

Wills rarely control all the assets.
The problems here are twofold: 1) How the assets are titled. See the sidebar titled "The Importance of Asset Titling" on page 5 for information about what's wrong with what seems like a common sense approach to titling your assets jointly. 2) How the beneficiaries are named. So, if you've named your spouse as the beneficiary of a life insurance policy, or even an IRA, that trumps anything your will may specify. How the assets are titled can also have significant impact on the real value of estate planning.

Wills don't work well across state lines.
For a will to work properly, it has to sync up with the laws in the state where you're domiciled at death. Here in Florida, thousands of people are perfectly happy with their wills that comply with the laws in New York, or Wisconsin, or Alaska. The problem is a will in one state may contain (or lack) terms that, in another state, trigger a different outcome.

Planning for the Intangibles

At the most basic level, wills and trusts are about stuff—who gets what and when and how. But what about the stuff that's not really stuff at all? We know who gets the house, but who gets the digital photos of all the memories the house contained?

Questions surrounding intangible digital assets are just beginning to be asked, much less answered. Estate planning in the Information Age raises a whole new set of issues that just didn't exist even five years ago. For example, who inherits the computer files, the web pages, blogs, and emails? More complicated yet, how are online bank accounts, stock holdings that exist entirely in digital media, or even the rights to an online profile to be handled? These digital holdings can have deep emotional value as well as considerable monetary value.

The dynamic nature of our digital lives and transactions makes it impractical, if not impossible, to include them accurately in a will. User names and passwords change, stocks are e-traded, and email accounts are established. It's not that the laws governing digital assets are unclear; it's that

(continued)

in most states they haven't even been written. Of course
that shouldn't stop you from writing your own rules.

First, keep a record of your significant online dealings
complete with user names and passwords. Keep it updated
and keep it safe.

Then make sure your attorney, estate executor, or
trustee is aware of the list. You don't have to show them;
just tell them where to look if you die or become ill and
then write to them about what you want to happen. It falls
short of "the law" but that doesn't mean it won't get done.
Digital assets don't exist in the same way a home or a boat
does, but they do take up space in your heart and even
your estate.

CREATE A LIVING WILL AND DESIGNATE A HEALTH CARE SURROGATE

Think of a Living Will as a gift to your family. It contains specific instructions to family members and medical professionals. If
you've been diagnosed with a terminal or end stage condition or
fall into a persistent vegetative state, your family and physicians
will know what you want. It's a heavy burden lifted in an already
anguishing experience. The laws vary from state to state; so, make
sure you have a Living Will that complies with the state in which
you are legally domiciled.

Your health care surrogate (sometimes called a medical power
of attorney) is essentially your health care agent—someone who
you authorize to make health care decisions if you can't and
only if you can't. These are difficult decisions to make, especially
since they often put your surrogate in opposition to a physician, such as having a physician removed or moving medical

care elsewhere. Make sure the person you designate understands what it means and can fight for you.

DESIGNATE, OR BE PREPARED TO DESIGNATE, AN ATTORNEY-IN-FACT

This is your agent on financial decisions. It's the person you delegate to manage assets and funding, as well as other legal matters like signing a tax return. A financial power of attorney document identifies both the "who" and the "what"—which powers they are granted and not granted. And then there's the "when."

The financial power of attorney can be "durable" or "springing." Durable powers remain in effect despite your subsequent disability. Springing powers only go into effect after there's a later determination that you are incapacitated. For each, there are advantages and risks, but that's a discussion best guided by you, your family, and your attorney.

The Importance of Asset Titling

Trusts won't fund themselves; they need to have assets "titled" to them or they are little more than hollow instruments that invite probate into your family. Funding a Revocable Living Trust (RLT) is a simple matter of changing title to the assets from your name to your name, as trustee, of your trust. And no, it can't wait until later.

A new client approached me with a net worth of $18 million and almost zero planning in place. He was 77 and I saw caution lights flashing. I recommended he start immediately with foundational planning, including the preparation and funding of a revocable living trust plus

(continued)

---

the purchase of a life insurance policy in an irrevocable trust to offset estate tax costs at the second of his and his wife's deaths—so the full value of his estate would pass to his heirs. He thanked me for my advice, but said he was heading from Florida to his northern home in Maine and would "think about it."

Two years later, I heard from his widow. Her husband had indeed established an RLT, but had neglected to fund it. The result was many months of probate, which drained substantial financial (and emotional) assets. It was "lengthy, expensive and worrisome." She also knew that probate could have been completely avoided if her husband had titled the assets to the trust. It was one mistake she was not going to make. She subsequently became a client and has retitled all of her assets into her name, as trustee of her RLT. Probate avoided, finally.

Mike Kilbourn

AVOID PROBATE COURT

It's a common misconception that a will and the health care directives mentioned above keep your estate out of probate. In fact, the opposite is true—the probate process exists in part to *verify the validity* of a will. In most states, probate is a dreadful experience that can drag on for months or even years. It's expensive (often 3 to 11 percent of the estate), it's public and, if contested, probate can bring out the worst in good people. If you have property in other states, then get set for "ancillary" probate in each state. When clients tell us what they absolutely *don't* want to happen, there's often a probate nightmare in their past.

The Foundational Planning corner in the Four Corners plan is structured to avoid probate altogether. That means moving from planning that's built around the will to planning that's built on trusts. And while there's a myriad of trust structures that can arise from the Four Corners plan, the footing for each is actually just one of two basic trust instruments.

TRUST IN TRUSTS

Revocable Living Trusts and Irrevocable Trusts are the two instruments at the foundation of much of what you'll read here. Underneath the alphabet of trust acronyms, there are really only these two kinds of trusts: Revocable and Irrevocable.

(And a trust? Think of it like a vault and only a few people know the combination. When assets are titled to an irrevocable trust they are "out of the estate" and safe from taxation and lawsuits.)

The Revocable Living Trust, or RLT, is the utility infielder of estate planning. It does many things very well and helps the entire line-up perform better. Much of what you'll see here as possibilities for your family have an RLT at their core. In addition to assets, an RLT also contains your specific wishes in the very same way that a will does. In effect, a properly structured RLT is your will.

Every RLT has a trustmaker (sometimes called a grantor or settlor), a trustee, and a beneficiary. And upon its creation, one person is usually all three. Depending on the jurisdiction and the specific circumstances, married couples may share a joint RLT or each person may have a separate RLT.

The central advantage to an RLT is contained in its middle name: It's living. RLTs allow you to maintain control of the assets placed under the trust. Since you are the initial trustee, you are the decision maker in how the assets are managed and when they are transferred in or out. Since you are the initial beneficiary, you profit from the gains created by the trust's assets.

Moreover, RLTs can keep your estate out of probate, include provisions for your disability, allow married couples to reduce estate taxes or avoid them altogether, and support a multitude of possibilities in how your estate passes to your heirs. You'll see a lot of Revocable Living Trusts in the pages ahead, but here's one way to think of them: When you're living, the trust is living and revocable. When you're not, it's not, and it becomes irrevocable.

Irrevocable Trusts, on the other hand, are typically created to last for more than one generation, often far more. And don't get hung up on the "irrevocable" part.

These trusts are less rigid than their name suggests. When properly structured, Irrevocable Trusts *can* be altered over time to reflect evolving circumstances and family dynamics, just not by you as grantor or the children named as beneficiaries, or even the trustee. Enter the protector, a fourth role that adds a measure of flexibility. More to follow on how protectors help families keep an estate aligned with the realities of life.

Rethinking Joint Tenancy

Joint tenancy with the right of survivorship is one of the most common and simplest forms of estate planning. It's also one of the riskiest. How it works: When the first of the joint tenants dies, the jointly owned assets pass to the other "tenant," effectively delaying probate on jointly owned assets until the death of the remaining owner. If the remaining joint tenant is your spouse, estate tax would not normally be due on jointly held property. Any estate tax due on these joint assets would be due at the remaining spouse's death. The risk in this approach is tied up in the shared responsibility for the assets.

Each joint tenant can be held responsible for actions of the other tenant. For example, titling an automobile jointly with a spouse or child who later becomes involved in an accident can cause you to be named as a defendant in a lawsuit resulting from that accident.

You could lose control of bank accounts, stock accounts, annuities, mutual funds, etc., because either joint tenant can liquidate or sell such assets without the permission or knowledge of the other owner. Also, if one joint owner has a problem with a creditor or judgment in a lawsuit, the other owner could lose the asset through court action or garnishment. Some jointly held property cannot be sold if one of the joint owners either cannot, because of illness, or will not sign.

Joint tenancy can also result in unintended disinheritance. For example, Tracy and Valerie both have children and grandchildren from previous marriages. If Tracy dies first and their property is held jointly, Valerie controls everything. That means she can leave the property to *her* heirs when she dies, thus disinheriting Tracy's children and grandchildren.

There may be gift tax implications. For example, one of my elderly neighbors, Louise, purchased a Florida condominium and titled it in her name and her stepdaughter's name as joint owners. By doing so, Louise also made a gift to her stepdaughter equal to 50 percent of the value of the home, potentially exposing herself to substantial gift taxes.

Another argument against joint tenancy: Beneficiaries receive the assets all at once, even when they may not be able to manage them. And jointly held assets may, upon the death of a joint owner, be immediately subject to the claims of the remaining owner's creditors.

Mike Kilbourn

CONSIDER A POUR OVER WILL

A Pour Over Will is a safety net for people who already have a revocable living trust, but die without transferring all of their assets to their trusts. It contains your wishes for property and assets not contained in trust. Those assets "pour over" to your trust, but not before going through probate. With good planning that stays current, there should be minimal, if any, assets subject to the Pour Over Will.

And the beneficiary is. . .?

It may have been years, or even decades ago, when you listed the beneficiary to that life insurance policy, annuity, or retirement account. It was a big decision then and it's a big issue now. Is that person still with us? Is she or he still your spouse? Did you identify a secondary or contingent beneficiary? When this simple item falls out of date, the consequences can be costly.

Mary purchased a Single Premium Life Insurance policy many years ago for $100,000 and named her husband, Howard, as the primary beneficiary with no secondary beneficiary. There would be time for that, after all, their daughter was just a baby. Many, many years later, Howard passed away and Mary neglected to update the beneficiary. When Mary died several years later, the life insurance death benefit was worth over $300,000, but because there was no named beneficiary, the proceeds were paid to Mary's estate after going through an expensive probate process. Had Mary updated the beneficiary to their daughter and, better yet, transferred ownership of the policy to an irrevocable trust, the life insurance death benefit would have passed without the grind of probate.

Robert O'Dell

Corner 2
Protection Planning

Nothing in life is to be feared. It is only to be understood.

Marie Curie

THERE ARE THREE IDEAS CENTRAL TO THIS CHAPTER. THE FIRST is keeping the wealth you've created robust and healthy. The second is keeping invasive species out. The third is a hybrid: protecting wealth within the family *from* the family, specifically certain members of the family that might be thinking less about your legacy and more about their immediate hungers, be they a shiny new Corvette or a fast exit from the family. The Protection Planning sector in the Four Corners plan serves all three.

As you consider the strategies and the broader emotional landscape of protection, a certain mindset is helpful: a mindset that's not fearful, but reasonably cautious—not aggressive, but proactive. The mindset is *vigilance*.

The word vigilance has its roots in the Latin term *vigilare* or, literally, "keep awake." Awake. That's a wonderful way to move through the most confounding area of estate planning: families. From the mythology of the Greeks through the books of the Bible, from Shakespeare to the Sopranos, humanity's better angels and brutish villains have lived side-by-side in the family tree. Remaining vigilant will help you serve your family's many angels without losing sleep over the occasional brute.

DEPLOY PROTECTION ON TWO FRONTS

The Four Corners plan is vigilant for you and your family right now, and your heirs years from now. In this chapter, you'll see a multitude of strategies as well as a few common instruments. Oddly enough, one of the most useful is also not particularly well liked: insurance. Insurance is something we all know is necessary but usually resist talking about, and that includes many estate planning and financial advisors. You resist it because insurance is too hypothetical, or too expensive, or you just don't like the industry. Financial advisors and estate planning attorneys often resist insurance for completely different reasons. That's not how it is around the Four Corners.

Insurance is, in many ways, the ultimate instrument for Protection Planning and you'll see some of the most steadfast below. They are all about protecting you and your family in the here-and-now where the hypothetical can become very real, very quickly. There's no good excuse for lacking adequate protection. But insurance, specifically life insurance, is also a dynamic tool for balancing estates and addressing challenges in how assets are structured. The language of insurance can be dense and the laws are complicated. Say what you want about the pushy insurance agent who chases people with his pitch, but insurance at its highest level is a financial service specialty that attracts some very smart people, people who are also paid very well for what they do. We don't have a problem with any of that, but many estate planning attorneys and financial advisors do. Insurance brokers and agents are paid large commissions at the time a policy is sold. Attorneys and advisors aren't, and too many of them let resentment get in the way of what's best for their clients. It's your legacy. Don't let petty feuds diminish it.

Income Replacement Insurance

For a family that is dependent on one or both of the spouses' paychecks to make ends meet, having an inadequate amount of disability and life insurance could be catastrophic.

Kevin and Becky are in their early 50s and at the peak of their spending cycle with two children in college, a sizable mortgage, and caring for elderly parents. They both have good careers earning sufficient income to meet their financial demands. However, in the event of a severe disability or premature death without proper disability and life insurance coverage, there could be lifestyle, even life-altering, consequences.

The amount of life insurance death benefit people should purchase to replace their income should be carefully determined after a detailed needs analysis. The needs analysis should take into account three different time periods the surviving spouse will likely experience:

- Caring for minor children
- Children out of the home and the spouse is not retired
- The surviving spouse is in retirement

Other factors that should be taken into account are other assets that will produce income, existing life insurance, debt, and realistic inflation assumptions.

Robert O'Dell

Protect the here-and-now

For readers who still draw a paycheck: Congratulations! You're healthy and working. It's also safe to assume that your continued income is important to the financial health of your family. You may even own the business that's paying you, which means your health is doubly important. We'll get to life insurance later, but let's assume that you have some. Great, but chances are you're not going to die this month or next. What's significantly more likely is you'll get injured or become sick. In that scenario, you're alive but you can't work or run the business. What now?

Disability coverage

If you're working, you need some disability coverage. Disability insurance typically replaces up to 60 percent of your annual earnings during the period of disability. The premium costs vary depending upon the inherent risks of your work and the level of income you need to replace. If you have an employer, find out what the policies are; our guess is, if there is any disability coverage at all, it's inadequate. If you are self-employed or run the business for your own income, it's simple: Protect yourself and your family.

Where's your umbrella?

Last year, the wife of a very close friend was involved in a serious traffic accident. She was broadsided at a stoplight when the other driver, a 90-year-old woman, failed to stop at the red light. Our friend had numerous injuries, especially to her arms and hands. In fact, doctors were unable to save several fingers. The other driver was uninjured and carried the state minimum insurance. Unfortunately, the liability limits fell short of the costs of prosthetics and physical therapy. So now, while recovering from the injuries, our friends are forced to seek damages from the woman at fault. It's a nightmare for everyone.

Would umbrella coverage make the injuries any less painful? No, but the pain of legal action is also very real and complicates the emotional landscape of physical therapy. I'm not casting blame; if either driver had an umbrella policy, then the financial hardships would be minimized, if not eliminated entirely.

Review your policies, imagine worst-case scenarios, and bring your coverage up to meet them.

Robert O'Dell

Long-Term Care coverage

A middle aged client said this: "I knew I was going to die. I just never thought I'd get old." Aging *can* surprise us, especially as the Baby Boom generation pushes back on Father Time with better habits and better science. Medical breakthroughs are indeed nudging the average lifespan upward. As people live longer, they also live further into the years when they need more care, and it's not just a geriatric issue. A serious accident or disabling illness can make long-term care a necessity at any age.

Many people are surprised when they realize that Medicare will not fully cover their long-term care costs. At best, Medicare will pay for all or part of the first 100 days of care and only if it follows a hospital stay to recuperate from an acute illness or injury. And that's *today's* Medicare. Care to guess what Medicare will cover in 20 years? You probably guessed less, which means you need to do more now.

The fact is that six out of ten people age 65 years or older will need at least one year of long-term care during their lifetime. The average annual cost for a private room in a nursing home is

approximately $80,000 and experts predict it will double in
15 years. It's heartbreaking, but not surprising, that failure to plan
for long-term care is the number one cause of poverty among
older Americans. The best way to be prepared for these costs, and
to protect your estate, is through long-term care insurance.

Umbrella coverage

Umbrella coverage is an extension of your home and auto insurance. It picks up where your liability begins and could be one
of the most important components in your protection portfolio.
Everyone should have umbrella coverage, and few actually do.
Why? The $100,000, $300,000 or, in some cases, $500,000 in
liability coverage that comes with most homeowner's policies,
at one time, sure looked reasonable, if not excessive. That may
have been a decade ago, or longer, when you actually reviewed
the liability limits. Or it could have been last week. But if you
think that's enough, you're living in another era. Our so-called
"litigious society" is real. Personal injury attorneys are prowling
for clients with half a case that can be settled out of court and
you never know what can come from a judge or jury, especially
when the defendant is in a neck brace. The truth is, bad accidents
do happen and people *are* injured or killed. If it's your fault, or
a family member's fault, it's already horrible enough; don't let it
destroy you financially.

The flip side, of course, is when an uninsured motorist
injures you or a family member. Or, for that matter, a motorist
with fully legal coverage that also happens to have liability limits
far below what you'll require to get better. An umbrella policy
can pay here too.

The good news is umbrella coverage is inexpensive, maybe
the best value in all of insurance. A million dollars in coverage
is usually the most expensive, maybe $200 to $400 a year. Each
additional million in coverage is around $100 to $200 annually.

Balance that with the devastation to your estate of a multi-million dollar legal judgment. Protect yourself.

Life insurance

At its most basic level, it replaces the income lost when the policyholder dies. There's no question that life insurance should be part of your portfolio while your family depends on your income. (See the sidebar titled "Income Replacement Insurance" on page 13 for starters.) In the pages that follow, you'll see how life insurance can be integrated into an enlightened estate plan, even if income replacement is a non-factor. Life insurance is like estate planning in at least one maddening way: The nomenclature can be impenetrable and off-putting. Whole life, universal life, variable life, indexed life—it's complex and can be expensive. Four Corners planning is open to all the advantages of life insurance, while acknowledging the cost trade-offs.

Now, let's expand the wall of protection and move from preserving the here-and-now to preserving your estate for the generations to follow.

Protect future generations

Protecting your estate so that it can enrich your heirs, and their heirs, is where Four Corners plans start to look much different than document-based planning. Documents organize *instruments*; Four Corners Protection strategies explore *possibilities*. Our conversations are about "what can be accomplished," not the "how" of drafting the docs. And just as two tree branches take different routes to reach the sunlight, there is no single path or strategy that fits each family. Some strategies overlap and can be combined in varying measures to align with individual preferences; some strategies can only be applied within specific situations and mandate precise actions in sequence. Each can be more intricate and nuanced than these pages are meant to contain. A thicker book isn't the answer either; textbooks and tax code manuals make poor listeners. That's the role of your estate plan advisors, whether our names are on the door or not. Your advisor's job is to learn about you and your family, to help you envision what's possible for each, and to craft a plan that strengthens your family tree for generations. Let's begin.

You can express devotion to your spouse and not let the IRS feel the love: the Estate tax exemption equivalent

Consider for a moment the "I love you" will. It can be a pretty simple document that explicitly states what you are passing to your spouse: ". . . and to my loving spouse, I pass everything— property, portfolio, personal stuff." Love is a wonderful thing and we're all for it, but this kind of will misses the first and easiest opportunity to keep assets out of your estate and out of Uncle Sam's hands: the Estate Tax Exemption Equivalent or, for our purposes, simply the "exemption." And the best analogy for it is the humble coupon.

Every American has one of these coupons except, instead of being worth 1/20th of a penny, this one is worth $5 million. Like every coupon, they're used at checkout: in this case, at the superstore of life. Sadly, it won't buy more time, but it can make life a lot better for everyone behind you in line. So, when you or your spouse arrives at the checkout, the IRS is standing there ready to cheerfully bag up the value of whatever assets are exposed to the estate tax. In the Four Corners plan, that's when the first $5 million coupon is used, which immediately removes that much from the oh-so-helpful hands of the revenuers. The balance of the estate is handed back to the remaining spouse in whatever form the inheritance takes. Because of what's called the "unlimited marital deduction," the IRS gets nothing, nor do they expect to at the first spouse's passing. That's because the

IRS is most interested in what the next shopper brings to the checkout—*that's* the estate that's ripe for taxation.

Estate planning that doesn't include the exemption is akin to poor judgment in the luxury aisle, because when the second-to-die spouse arrives at checkout—let's say it's the wife—she can't simply pull out both her and her husband's coupon for a $10 million exemption. Because like all coupons, it's one per customer.

The $5 million that was saved by using the coupon at the first death can be placed into what's called a Family Trust. For married couples, it's a basic benefit of a revocable living trust and it's created to house the first exemption. The remainder of the estate passes to your spouse *without* being pre-loaded with unnecessary estate taxes due. Family Trusts are good ideas for several reasons, including protection of the assets and keeping any appreciation out of the remaining spouse's estate. But that's not the only option.

Thanks to the Tax Relief, Unemployment Insurance Reauthorization, and Job Creation Act of 2010, the unused portion of the exemption is portable, meaning it can move to the surviving spouse (i.e., if the husband dies and uses $4 million of his credit, when his wife dies, she can use her $5 million credit plus her husband's remaining $1 million). All of which actually takes the coupon out of the picture—for now. This shift in tax law is subject to repeal or revision in the next legislative session, or the next, or the next. It can change and, if experience is any guide, it *will* change eventually. Besides, it's simply good Protection Planning to move $5 million into a trust where it can appreciate securely versus handing it to a spouse where it's exposed to the unknown and unknowable. That's why the exemption—the coupon—should stay in your pocket and be used in every situation.

OK, marriage can be a good thing in the Four Corners plan, but lowering taxes is only the beginning of what you can do.

You can keep the tax collector and other parasites away from the estate your spouse is passing to your children: Qualified Terminable Interest Property Trusts

If it's a first marriage, you have two groups of family to consider—the first is your spouse (OK, it's a small group), the second is your children and other heirs, which could be an actual group. Of course you want your spouse to live comfortably on your estate, drawing income from assets left outright or in trust and, if needed, from the Family Trust. But if the estate is likely to be taxable at your spouse's death—meaning if there will be more than $5 million—there's a way you can secure your spouse's share of the estate *and* make sure that your children inherit what's left. That's called a QTIP trust.

A Qualified Terminable Interest Property trust simply puts a wall around the assets, protecting them for your spouse's use now and for your children when she, or he, departs. The spouse collects the income from the QTIP and can even have access to the principal for "health, education, maintenance, and support." It's all spelled out when the trust is crafted and you have many options. The key takeaway is QTIP assets qualify for the unlimited marital deduction and pass under his or her estate tax exemption and yet you decide who receives the remaining assets. It's not about restricting your spouse's access to the estate; it's about protecting your children's inheritance from gold diggers and other parasites.

Harmony in a second marriage

This is a big category with a lot of variation from one situation to the next. Some second marriages produce children, some don't. Some grown children are delighted to see mom and/or dad find someone to love. And some are, let's say, less than enthusiastic. As you can imagine, the epicenter of family drama in second and third marriages is the estate.

The good news is an estate plan can be crafted to dial down the fear and resentment, while creating win/win outcomes for everyone. Who knows, you might one day see the whole clan sitting together at the Thanksgiving table, genuinely thankful to be there.

The misunderstood mission of a premarital agreement

Premarital agreements get a bad rap yet, like so many things we're leery of, they're really just *misunderstood*. It's true that many long-term couples can talk about sex more easily than they can money—even when it's *their* money. When it's "my money *not* your money," the room can get awfully quiet. That's our cue to say something helpful.

In these pages you're discovering new ways to *think* about your estate; they can also guide you in how to *talk* about your estate with everyone you love—your heirs *and* your sweetheart. So, let us count the ways the pre-nup is misunderstood.

Premarital agreements tarnish romance with mistrust.

Mistrust around money is more likely to follow unspoken expectations than clear and honest communication. Forget the document; it's about sharing what's important to you and the legacy you envision. Your ideas for how the estate can support your family's success shouldn't be expected to fit into a single, awkward conversation or, worse, an unexpected document that's waiting next to breakfast one morning.

Premarital agreements invite lawyers to where there should be love.

Marriage itself is an institution formalized by a legal agreement. The ceremony may have the majesty of a big church or the convenience of a Las Vegas drive-thru chapel, but the marriage is a marriage because two people signed a legal document. A well-crafted premarital agreement simply spells out some financial specifics after "I do."

Premarital agreements make a future divorce more likely.
Now this would be interesting data: What are the divorce rates in marriages with premarital agreements? And, more importantly, how do those divorce rates compare with the divorce rates of marriages where the financial situations were roughly the same, but there were no premarital agreements in place? Our experience shows us that premarital agreements relieve tension and create emotional space for deepening the best parts of a relationship.

Premarital agreements are one-sided.
This misunderstanding misses a critical fact: It's an agreement between two people who love each other. That's not sweet talk either; it's real. We've seen agreements that are as protective of the spouse as of the wealth. In one agreement, if the marriage lasts for at least three years, our client's future wife would receive a $1 million lump-sum payment, the house, the car and most living expenses paid in full for life. The wife felt respected and secure, and a multi-million dollar family business was protected from a messy divorce. And guess what? 14 years later, they are still married and as in love today as they were when they signed the agreement.

Premarital agreements create pressure to sign.
They better not, because if the agreement was signed under duress (an hour before the wedding, for example), a judge can toss it out. As of this writing, 27 states have adopted the Uniform Premarital Agreement Act. The act defines procedures and rules meant to keep these agreements fair—from asset disclosure to

timing. On the Four Corners website, there's an up-to-date list-
ing of states that have adopted the act and links to sites where
you can learn more.

*Premarital agreements are between two people in the
here-and-now.* They don't have to be. Here's where we jump forward in time
and imagine a scenario in which there's a surviving spouse with
a sizable estate. As the years pass, he or she may want to remarry.
Good for them, but a Four Corners plan can also make sure it's
good for the rest of the family and here's where a premarital
agreement comes in: It's *not* between you and a future spouse.
It's between your surviving spouse and his or her spouse-to-be.
How's that possible?

   This kind of future premarital agreement specifies that if the
surviving spouse remarries, the new spouse must sign a premarital agreement. Call it Gold Digger Repellent; it protects the sur-
vivor's portion of the estate, as well as your heirs'. It also saves the
surviving spouse the anxiety of talking about a premarital agreement in personal terms: "It's not my idea. This is how my late
husband/wife wanted it. It's about our family, not about you."

   Of course, the new spouse can refuse to sign it and the surviving spouse is free to marry anyone. But with no agreement,
the surviving spouse walks away from the distributions and
whatever control was granted as trustee. Either way, you know
the new spouse won't be marrying for money.

When premarital assets are dramatically different

It's not uncommon to have clients remarry later in life with a
wide difference in their respective net worth. And the most common is the older husband with a high net worth and a younger
wife—she's got a zest for life, but her net worth is effectively zero.
This couple isn't going to have children, so the husband would

like to pass the lion's share of his estate to his children and grand-children, *and* minimize the estate tax hit when it passes to his heirs. A good premarital agreement spells out the legal ownership of the husband's assets. But what if she dies first, with little wealth in her name still? Can they still use her estate tax exemption? Indeed they can, IF they've planned well. It's another kind of QTIP trust, a lifetime QTIP.

A lifetime QTIP can be set up in the wife's name to contain an amount equal to the estate tax exemption, $5 million. In the unlikely event that she dies first, the estate has a full estate tax deduction on the books and those dollars return to the husband in a Family Trust, ready to pass tax-free to his heirs at his death. And if she outlives her husband—the more likely scenario—she's got income and some access to the trust funds for the rest of her life (it's all spelled out when the QTIP is set up). And then, when she dies, the full balance of the QTIP goes to the husband's heirs, tax-free.

You can put much of your estate in trust and still preserve some "just in case" control: Spousal Estate Reduction Trusts

It's generally a good idea to move assets out of your estate, especially when there's no doubt that those assets will not be needed to support your spouse's lifestyle after you're gone. But what if you're not so certain? Or what if you simply don't feel comfortable giving it to the children, even in trust? Well, there's a trust for you and your spouse.

A Spousal Estate Reduction Trust (SERT) allows you to name your children and grandchildren as the remainder beneficiaries, but during your spouse's lifetime he or she will still have access to the income and principal—but not so much access that the assets are considered to be in his or her name. A SERT is ideal for families who have just entered the territory where their wealth requires planning to avoid or minimize estate taxes.

You can leverage the tax-free status of life insurance to protect and pass on a full range of trust assets: Irrevocable Life Insurance Trusts

Life insurance is the one truly tax-free investment. All other investments can be subject to income or capital gains tax. Qualified retirement plans and annuities are tax deferred—not tax-free. Even the "no-tax" municipal bonds are essentially "pre-taxed" via their lower rates of return. This isn't news; even people who aren't CPAs or financial advisors understand that when a life insurance policy pays, the IRS can't get their hands on it. Their hands, however, still can find ways to reach into your pocket. Because what's less well known is that the *proceeds* from life insurance policies owned at death will be included in their estate for estate tax purposes. Since the policy owner can withdraw the cash value and change the beneficiary, the policy owner has control or *"incidents of ownership"* over the proceeds which can then be taxed at death. Not to worry; there's a strategy that protects the proceeds of life insurance.

An Irrevocable Life Insurance Trust, or ILIT for short, is an irrevocable trust specifically designed to hold and own life insurance policies and their proceeds outside of the taxable estate and out of the reach of creditors and lawsuits. Of course, ILITs are merely instruments. They need to be integrated in the proper way to protect and enrich your estate. In a Four Corners plan, an ILIT is the core of another planning acronym, SLAT. Much like the SERT discussed earlier, a Spousal Lifetime Access Trust does pretty much what it sounds like: It gives your spouse lifetime access to the assets of a trust—an ILIT. The ILIT grows on the increased cash value of the policy and other assets that are titled to the trust—including non-liquid assets, like property. When you're alive, the ILIT's trustee (usually the spouse of the insured) can access and distribute the policy's cash value and any other assets as specified by the trust document. After you've died, the death benefit is paid to the ILIT, which can then make distributions to your spouse, children, and other beneficiaries. ILIT funds can even lend money to beneficiaries and purchase assets from the estate. SERTs and ILITs, like so many of the high-functioning strategies on these pages, require expert guidance to establish and maintain. It takes some time and requires a few more bucks than a simple insurance premium check. But then again, you didn't build your estate overnight either.

You can pass your estate to your children and then protect it as it passes to your grandchildren and beyond: Generation Skipping Trusts and Dynasty Trusts

For legacy-minded readers, we're getting into the good stuff—how a plan can be fitted with the ability to span generations. But first, here's another quick lesson in the upside down world of trust nomenclature. The instrument that makes this strategy so appealing is called a Generation Skipping Trust (GST) or sometimes a Dynasty Trust. GSTs are designed to benefit more than one generation and do not necessarily skip any of your heirs. GSTs "skip" paying estate taxes as assets pass from one generation to the next. It may sound mean and even reckless, but no one is left out and everyone can win, except, of course, the tax collector. "IRS skipping trust" is a name we can all appreciate.

GSTs are planning strategies that followed the Generation Skipping Transfer Tax, which was implemented by the IRS when it thought that too many wealthy families were using smart planning to avoid both gift and estate taxes from generation to generation. Essentially, Uncle Sam was being skipped, and you know that wasn't going to go on forever. Speaking of forever, meet the Dynasty Trust.

When to terminate a trust? Try 360 years.

State laws dictate how long assets can remain in trust. In some states, it's forever; in Florida, it's 360 years. Nearly the same thing, right? I recommend trusts be set up for as long as the state allows. Every year I hear another story of a trust with a termination clause based on when the beneficiary reaches a certain age. If the trust is well-crafted, the beneficiary can have access to the income and to the principal when needed for health, education, maintenance, and support. It's doing everything a trust should do, so why terminate it? Maybe the grantor thought 40 sounded like an age when the beneficiary would be building a solid, stable life. Did the grantor see the divorce that was looming and envision a conversation like this?

> Trustee: You're 40 now. We're ready to send your check.
>
> Beneficiary: Wait, I'm in the middle of an ugly divorce from a truly despicable person!
>
> Trustee: (Pause) Would you like us to divide it now and send a check to each of you?

Even when the termination delivers dollars to a healthy person in a happy life, it arrives naked and exposed—the trust protection is gone and those assets are now vulnerable to all the unfortunate circumstances of life.

The moral: Let a trust do what it does best for as long as it legally can. Your heirs will thank you, maybe even those who are hundreds of years in the future.

Mike Kilbourn

A Dynasty Trust is essentially a GST without a defined end point. Some states have laws that prevent an estate from passing on in perpetuity, but they've set the finish line far, far into the future—360 years in Florida. When we mention dynasty trusts, clients can be mortified: "We don't want to rule over our future heirs like some manipulative monarch." You won't. A properly structured Dynasty Trust in a Four Corners plan helps create legacies, not dynasties. Here's how:

No one owns the assets so your heirs can leverage the income

With these trusts, the assets never actually pass to their named beneficiaries. (Or, in states with long time horizons or no limit on how long a trust may last, it can be several generations before the assets are distributed.) Your children are likely the first beneficiaries, then their children, then their children. All along, each generation avoids or reduces estate and gift taxes that are triggered at the passing from your estate to theirs, and then to their children and to their children and so on.

Think about it: 100 years from now, one dollar in a GST/Dynasty trust earning just 6 percent will grow to almost $340. But these trusts are more than object lessons in the power of compounding interest; they're also income-generating instruments that grow with the generations *and* are legally protected from creditors, a divorcing spouse, or an asset-seeking personal injury lawyer. This fact alone makes GSTs and Dynasty trusts powerful instruments for families across the asset spectrum. Like so many ideas in this book, these were created for the ultra-wealthy but they function beautifully for families with big dreams and more modest estates.

Legacies underway: putting the money to work

When the grantor (you) creates a GST or a Dynasty trust, the income distribution to the beneficiaries is also spelled out. It's often in the form of a fixed annual percentage that's paid from the trust monthly. If the amount falls short of what's needed for "health, support, maintenance, and education," and the beneficiary doesn't have other income available, the trustee has the discretion to make additional payments from principal. The trustee can also loan money to the beneficiary for business ventures or to pursue an advanced degree. The options are many, unfolding decade after decade as the trust grows. But if the trust, not the kids, owns the assets, who is minding the trust?

Trustees and other defenders of your legacy

Since a dynasty trust can, at least theoretically, last forever, the initial trustee should also be named to administer it forever. So until medical science figures out how to keep people alive and on their toes forever, that may mean a corporate trustee—they're bound by fiduciary regulations, they provide professional investment and asset management services, and they're going to stay abreast of changes in the law that could damage the trust's ability to help the beneficiaries succeed.

A corporate trustee remains neutral, which is a clear advantage when the trust is shared by multiple beneficiaries, but also a disadvantage when it comes to fostering a sense of autonomy and self-determination among your heirs. In fact, we've seen some families in active rebellion against the corporate trustee who had let the autocratic aspects of a dynasty creep into how they administered the dynasty trust. But even the most perceptive trustee lacks a deep understanding of the heart and soul of a family. One alternative? More family.

Co-trustees

Dynasty trusts can be established so that trust beneficiaries serve as co-trustees. One possibility is having one or more members from each generation of beneficiaries over 25 years old serve as a co-trustee. That empowers the family co-trustees to share in decisions about the trust asset allocation or how and when to loan money from the trust. They also take responsibility for replacing or removing a co-trustee who has lost the ability or desire to perform in that role. There's no doubt that family co-trustees make administration more complex—technically and emotionally—but they may give the trust a more accurate reflection of your family.

Trust protectors
Here's a specific example of an estate planning idea that has moved from the ultra wealthy to merely the ultra smart and has become a common strategy in a Four Corners plan: trust protectors. Trust protectors have long been associated with trusts housed in foreign countries—they kept an eye on the local regulations and had authority to remove the foreign trustee or even relocate the trust. Here on the mainland, trust protectors are generally defined as having specific power over the trust or the trustee, but with no day-to-day fiduciary responsibilities. They can be the family CPA or a group of individuals who serve as a kind of board of directors. If you're reading between the lines here, you're seeing a lot of ambiguity. That's because the law in most states hasn't caught up with the industry so trust protectors can be named to do just about anything outside the fiduciary role of administering the trust.

They can remove and replace a trustee. The most common—often the only—power of trust protectors is the ability to replace a trustee or co-trustee who is unresponsive to the needs of the beneficiaries or who is not performing to the standard required by the trust's stated investment policy.

They can be the referee. Protectors can resolve deadlocks between co-trustees or even serve as an in-house arbitrator to help resolve big disputes between the beneficiaries and the trustee, potentially reducing the trust's litigation costs.

They can amend the trust.   A protector with this authority gives the trust more flexibility to make changes in beneficiary distributions or to add beneficiaries. It allows the trust to change with changing laws—especially important for long-term trusts.

They can change the trust's address.   The legal home of a trust determines which state's tax laws will apply, an important factor in its administration. For example, some states tax beneficiaries' trust income at higher rates. A trust protector can be responsible for moving the trust's legal home to a more favorable state.

What can't they do?   A trust protector can't make a single decision from self-interest. They are neutral actors in the plan and they can only make decisions that serve the trust.

The Vital Role of the Trust Protector

In trust law, a protector is one or more persons or entities appointed under a trust instrument to direct or restrain the trustees in relation to their administration of the trust. A protector should be someone who will act in the long-term interest of the beneficiaries, but cannot be the grantor, a trustee, or beneficiary under the trust.

Although the position of protector has been in the law for many years, it is surprising how few estate planning professionals bring up the subject in estate planning discussions. With so many things that could change over time, including tax law revisions, it seems prudent to always name a protector in irrevocable trusts.

(continued)

Depending upon the powers granted, a trust protector can add an additional layer of flexibility and protection that often represents the balance of power between the trust, the trustee, the grantor, and the beneficiaries.

- Protectors allow a great deal of flexibility when dealing with changes in circumstances, such as death, divorce, health issues, and tax law.
- The grantor may wish to withhold certain powers from the trustees.
- The grantor could have a protector act as a main point of contact between the beneficiaries and the trustee.

The powers vested in the protector can be limited, such as making adjustments relating to tax law changes, or much broader and include such things as the power to:

- Remove and appoint trustees
- Add or remove beneficiaries
- Approve trust distributions
- Control spending over a certain amount
- Resolve deadlocks between co-trustees
- Change the trust's situs to take advantage of state tax laws, etc.
- Veto or approve investment decisions
- Sue and defend lawsuits against trust assets
- Approve the appointment of an agent or advisor generally or relative to specific matters
- Appoint replacement protectors
- Terminate the trust or approve the termination of the trust

> Since the trust protector's role is created to add an additional layer of protection, it is important to choose a person familiar with your long-term personal and financial goals. It is not unusual to name your attorney in this role, but you might also consider naming your CPA, a sibling who is not a beneficiary, or even one or more close friends.
>
> *Mike Kilbourn*

Non-conventional planning for non-traditional families

When it comes to defining what a family is, estate laws tend to look like a lot of other U.S. laws—they default to the norms of a man married to a woman and both of them are U.S. citizens. OK, fine. But your estate *planning* shouldn't default to anything except you and your family. Here are two situations we've often seen:

Unmarried partners

This one is easy. First, review the Foundational Planning corner in the Four Corners plan and make sure you have established the advanced directives and powers of attorney. Then, review how you have your various assets titled. If they are titled in both names, then the law will likely consider them shared assets and expose the surviving partner to gift or estate taxes. The Four Corners approach here is to title the assets to the person who earned them, then build a plan that assures the assets pass to the partner.

An unmarried partner of any flavor, heterosexual or same sex, can be named as a beneficiary in life insurance, a standard will, or a trust. In fact, of all the estate planning options available to families, only the unlimited marital deduction is unavailable to unmarried couples. Marriage can be a wonderful thing, but it shouldn't be the only path to an enlightened estate plan.

Your non-citizen spouse

Marriage simplifies some aspects of passing an estate, but the benefits are not evenly applied across the matrimonial landscape. For transfers to and from non-citizen spouses, the estate tax exemption is not *automatically* available, nor is the unlimited marital deduction, which presents a real challenge for estates that might have avoided or postponed the estate tax if the full exemption and marital deduction had been available. If your spouse is not a U.S. citizen, you're going to need a guide because it's not an easy road. First stop: gifts.

Gifts are a viable estate planning strategy for all kinds of people and we'll explore them more in the next section. Gifts that would result in no taxes when given to a citizen spouse can generate significant taxes when given to a non-citizen spouse. What's a gift? Just about everything, even if you don't consider it a gift. For example, when you buy a home with a non-citizen spouse and title the home in joint tenancy, you may have just handed him or her a big tax bill in the future. What can be done instead?

One option is citizenship. If the non-citizen spouse takes the plunge and earns the U.S. citizen badge, then the unlimited exemption and marital deduction is back in the planning toolkit. The good news: Citizenship doesn't have to be granted before the citizen spouse dies. The non-citizen spouse has until the estate of the deceased must file the estate tax return, that's nine months with a six month extension possible. But citizenship isn't for everyone, that's why there's the QDOT, a Qualified Domestic Trust.

Remember above how "automatically" was emphasized with the estate tax exemption? A QDOT is manual transmission—there's some skilled clutching and shifting required, but a well-crafted QDOT allows a non-citizen spouse to postpone payment of estate taxes. All the income of the QDOT must be paid to the surviving spouse (subject to income tax but not estate tax). When the non-citizen spouse dies, Uncle Sam gets paid and any remaining principal is distributed as directed in the trust document, usually to the children.

Protecting and planning for families with special needs

Parents and grandparents of children with special needs face unique challenges, both in providing for the children while both parents are alive as well as providing for them after both parents are deceased. This is true whether the special needs children are 5 or 55. Estate planning for these families shares one fundamental objective: assure adequate care throughout the lifetime of the special needs family member, without disqualifying them from government assistance.

In medicine, the first rule is to do no harm. So it is with planning for the requirements of a family member with special needs. Parents (and grandparents) should resist leaving assets to the special needs child in a will, establishing custodial accounts, or setting up non-specialized trusts. Each can do harm, because the inevitable distribution of assets may disqualify them from government assistance, including Supplemental Security Income (SSI).

Special Needs Trust

Even if an adult with special needs qualifies for SSI and Medicaid, the benefits provided are limited. With most of the SSI benefit used for food and shelter, few, if any, financial resources are left for anything more. Medicaid covers medical care and prescription drugs, but not dental work. The goal, then, is to provide for those extras without disqualifying for government assistance. And for that, there's the Special Needs Trust.

A Special Needs Trust can provide distributions only for those extra needs and are made at the discretion of a *disinterested* trustee. Authorized distributions may include dental expenses, special schooling, even travel expenses. In fact, almost any expense not covered through government benefits can be paid through a Special Needs Trust. Upon the death of the beneficiary, the remaining trust assets may be administered on behalf of other family members.

Blended Discretionary Trust

It's tempting to simply leave an inheritance to another relative, with the understanding that it is to be used to supplement the needs of the family member with special needs. That's harmful too. That relative may lack the morals to honor the obligation or may become disabled in an accident. He or she could lose the inheritance through divorce, lawsuit, or bankruptcy. If they die, the inherited assets may be exposed to estate taxes. One alternative is the Blended Discretionary Trust.

These trusts offer the standard asset protection of trusts, but instead of specific beneficiaries and specific distribution instructions, Blended Discretionary Trusts have multiple beneficiaries, each with no specific right to any distribution of income or principal from the trust assets. It's vital that the trustee is truly independent and disinterested, but they can be guided by your wishes in a detailed, but non-binding, letter.

Payback Trust

Sometimes a disabled person who receives government benefits is named to receive an inheritance in a manner that would disqualify them from receiving needed benefits. Instead of simply disqualifying them, the federal government made it possible to establish a trust to administer and distribute trust assets for a beneficiary with special needs. However, as the name implies, there are strings attached—special provisions that require the trust to pay back the government for benefits provided to the trust beneficiary after his or her death. If trust assets are depleted or are otherwise insufficient to fully repay the government, no further reimbursement is required. However, if trust assets remain after the payback, the remaining assets may be distributed to additional beneficiaries designated under the trust.

Funding the trusts

Every trust needs cash inside it and each of the trusts mentioned above can be funded through gifts, non-liquid assets titled to the trust, and life insurance—either by naming the trust as beneficiary or by creating an ILIT to house all the assets.

USING GIFTS TO CREATE LEGACIES

Gifts to family members are like real-time legacy building. They receive their inheritance in manageable increments and you manage to steadily reduce your estate tax bill. There are several strategies that make the most of gifts and one of the easiest to implement is to simply double it.

You see, every taxpayer can give away up to $13,000 each year to as many people as they wish (as of 2012). That's known as the AGE, or Annual Gift Exclusion. Now double it. That's gift splitting and it means that you and your spouse may give a total of $26,000 each year to an unlimited number of individuals without triggering the gift tax. It doesn't matter who had the money in the first place and gifts that total less than $13K annually don't trigger gift taxes. So, there's AGE and then there's a *lifetime*.

In addition to transfers under the Annual Gift Exclusion, taxpayers are able to make total lifetime tax-exempt transfers of wealth totaling $5,120,000 (as of 2012) independent of the AGE limitations. If you have two grandkids, you and your spouse can make their lives over five million dollars better and your estate more than ten million dollars lighter. But there's a warning light blinking: The grandkids' gifts are received at the cost basis and any asset appreciation over the original cost basis will trigger capital gains taxes when the assets are sold. That's an inefficient gift. Good planning can ensure that you make gifts as efficiently as possible.

Gifts aren't right for every estate or every family, but once you make the decision to integrate gifts into your estate plan, there are several ways to wrap the packages, beginning with no wrapping at all.

Outright gifts

An outright gift has no strings attached. It's the simplest *and* the most reckless because once the gift is out of your hands, it's also exposed to the bad things that can happen, even to good kids. Divorce, lawsuits, and bankruptcy can target the gift assets. And then there's life—a young person with a lot of money and a lack of restraint can blow through sizable gifts like they were candles on a birthday cake.

Custodial accounts

Custodial accounts are gifts with a tag that reads "Do not open until you're 18" (or 21, depending on the state). These are popular alternatives because without much administrative effort, they create the illusion of a cautious wealth exchange. True, the dollars aren't in the family member's hands until he or she is a legal adult. But crossing an age threshold like 18 or 21 doesn't automatically confer wisdom or discretion. They're just as likely to get into a new car as a college dorm room.

Crummey trusts

It's an unfortunate name for an otherwise savvy option. The name derives from a 1968 court case, Crummey v. Commissioner. It's a fascinating case for students of estate law, but here's the summary: Crummey won. Now, so can you and your heirs. Here's how:

First, create a trust agreement that specifies how you want the assets to be managed and identify a trustee to administer the trust. Second, make lifetime gifts, within your annual gift exclusion, to the trust on behalf of your trust beneficiary (or beneficiaries). Third, the trustee provides written notice to the beneficiary (or their legal guardian) each time you make a gift *and* gives the beneficiary a period of time (typically 30 days) to exercise their right to withdraw some or all of the gifted amount. That's right: some or all.

Then, if the beneficiary does not exercise this withdrawal right, the trustee administers the gift for the beneficiary according to your original specifications. By keeping the assets in trust, they are out of your estate and protected from bad people and bad decisions. Of course, that's what all trusts do. Crummey trusts also give your heirs the opportunity to take control of their inheritance in modest chunks—if they blow it, you're free to stop gifting into the trust. If they make good decisions (including the brilliant decision to keep the money working for them), then you've gained some valuable insight into their maturing character and can continue to gift in confidence.

If properly structured and administered, a Crummey trust allows you to use your annual gift tax exclusion, even though the intent is to have the assets remain in trust for future benefit. Take note: Crummey trusts aren't the easiest to set up and administer. They require precise communication and ongoing attention to detail. But those efforts can pay off dramatically with heirs who learn how to manage their growing wealth as they grow in responsibility and self-knowledge. Thank you, Mr. Crummey.

MANAGE A FAMILY BUSINESS AND
THE BUSINESS OF FAMILY

Now we shift into a higher level of planning. When there's a business in the family, or when managing the family's assets is a business unto itself, the plan scales up with the dollars—and with the risks. It begins with a shift in your own thinking.

Use a Family Limited Partnership to control what you don't own

Some planning solutions appear to defy the laws of financial physics. After all, isn't owning an asset the same as controlling an asset? Most of the time, yes, but there are exceptions. Enter the FLP or Family Limited Partnership.

Family Limited Partnerships began as strategies for the super affluent. Today they're used by all kinds of families seeking a better way to manage their wealth, lower their taxes, and pass on a greater share of their estate. FLPs aren't for every family and, frankly, not every advisor is capable of crafting a legally sound FLP. Yet, for those families that do have the right blend of assets, advisors, and a willingness to take their thinking to a new level, an FLP can be a very comfortable place to live and work. Here's how it works:

Once a limited partnership has been formed and legally recognized, assets that were initially owned by one or two people, typically the husband and wife, are re-titled so that the FLP owns the assets. Assets that were owned by the heirs can also be titled to the FLP. And the family owns the FLP as share-owning partners.

The partners are identified in one of two categories—general partners and limited partners. General partners (GPs) are typically the source of the original assets. Limited partnership "shares" are often gifted to the heirs, making them the Limited Partners (LPs). And here's where it get's interesting: While a majority of the shares are gifted to the LPs, the *controlling* shares remain under the GP's control. Ownership and control are effectively separated. The LPs own it; the GPs control it. The GPs make the management decisions on the FLP assets and, when the FLP assets generate income, the GPs can be entitled to compensation for their management services.

And the LPs? Like the label says, their partnership power is limited. They can't make investment decisions, decide when to make distributions, force the partnership to buy their interests, or dissolve the partnership. They can't even sell or transfer their shares without the permission of the GPs. They may, at the discretion of the GP, receive distributions of the partnership income, but they don't have control, and that's a good thing. Because the shares have no marketability, the shares are *discounted* in value and it's those discounts that allow larger gifts of wealth and estate planning to reduce gift and estate taxes. Here's an example:

Dave and Peg jointly own $1 million in real estate, stocks, bonds, etc. With the intent of adding a layer of protection and making gifts of their assets, they create a Limited Partnership and receive all the GP and LP shares. If Dave and Peg give away 2.6 percent of the assets *outright* to each child, that would be $26,000 to each child. This amount is within the current gift tax exemption of $13,000 per recipient ($26,000 if the parents "split" the gift). If, however, they fund the partnership with the $1 million of assets and give away limited partnership shares, after a 40 percent valuation discount is applied, the parents could effectively give a total of $43,333 to each child and have it count as a split gift of $26,000. This way Dave and Peg are able to give away more assets, shifting wealth out of their estate. This strategy is particularly effective when the estate is too large to be reduced through gifts intended to fit within the annual gift tax exemption limits.

In a Family Limited Partnership, parents can begin to shift wealth to their children, introduce them to asset management, educate them about investments and wealth, and facilitate and manage pooled resources. FLPs are effective in spreading illiquid assets or assets of diverse valuations and marketability across a group of heirs.

What's more, the GP/LP orientation above can be flipped. Children can also manage their parents' assets through an FLP instead of a trust. In this application, the children are the general partners and the parents are the limited partners. The parents own a greater share of the assets and, thus, receive most of the income stream, but the children manage the assets for the parents. Upon the parents' death, those assets can be discounted and distributed without going through probate, assuming of course that the shares are titled to the RLT.

Be a pig, not a hog

You may be wondering, "What could possibly go wrong?" Well, quite a bit, beginning with the discount. You may have heard the phrase, "Pigs eat. Hogs get slaughtered." It should be the unofficial motto of every FLP. An FLP is able to take a discount if properly structured under state law and backed up with a valuation, but the question from an IRS auditor will be, "How much is too much?" Typically, discounts in the 25–35 percent range are taken. It's possible to justify a 60 percent discount or more, and it's also possible that some hoggish greed has pushed up to the trough. Here are a few questions to ask your inner hog:

Why did you set up the FLP?   If it's just a tax reduction play, you're starting to stink. The key is to have a legitimate business interest—beyond the estate tax-reducing discounts—for setting up the FLP. Maybe it's combining the collective wealth of a family to gain access to better managers. Operating an illiquid asset like a family business or a portfolio of buildings is classic FLP.

When was the FLP established? Setting up a partnership and funding it on a terminally ill parent's deathbed paints a target on your fat hog butt. The IRS would almost certainly ignore the claimed discounts.

What do you do with the FLP once established? To be seen as legitimate, an FLP needs to be run as a true business. This means segregating assets, regular meetings, policies and procedures—the stuff of a functioning business. Poor business administration isn't just lazy—to the IRS it's greedy.

Consider using a Limited Liability Company

A Limited Liability Company (LLC) or a Family Limited Liability Company (FLLC) can serve as an alternative to an FLP or in combination with an FLP. The two have a number of similarities and a few important differences. These differences may add up to advantages for some families or for certain types of assets.

How they are similar:
- Distinct tiers of LLC ownership can be established with a management class and a non-management class.
- The transfer of ownership interests can be limited to family members.
- LLCs/FLLCs are entitled to the same lack-of-control and marketability discounts that apply to FLPs.

How they are different and, perhaps, better:
The central advantage of an LLC is revealed in its name. It limits liability for each member, not just the named GPs and LPs. Personal assets of *all* the owners of the LLC are protected from business liability. Typically, an LLC will be used to hold and shield individual assets, such as real estate, boats, airplanes, and other potential liability-generating assets.

While the Limited Partners of an FLP cannot participate in management, members of an LLC are able to fully participate in management without sacrificing liability protection.

Pass on a successful business, even when some of your kids want nothing to do with it

Let's say you've poured your life into a business that's now on solid footing and growing. The value of that business may in fact be the bulk of your estate. One of your three kids has been there for years, helping to increase the value and preparing to take the reins. Your other two kids? No, thank you. They appreciate your hard work and they may have even spent a few years toiling at your side, but they are onto different lives. They don't want the business and the one who's running it probably doesn't want them moving into the front office. What now?

First, put down the phone; there's no need to call the business broker. Selling a $30 million business just to pass $10 million to each child is akin to the absurd Vietnam-era tactic of "destroying the village in order to save it." Another conventional approach is to send your son or daughter who's in the business in search of financing to buy the business from you, which may or may not deliver the dollars needed to pass the estate in a way that's fair to all. This sounds like a job for The Equalizer, a.k.a. life insurance.

Earlier in this chapter we explored the multiple advantages of life insurance and specifically the ILIT, or Irrevocable Life Insurance Trust. For business owners the advantages go even deeper by providing instant liquidity to pass on the value of a business to non-participating heirs without having to liquidate the business. The benefit can also pay the estate taxes due, letting the family get back to building a business that's a family legacy, not an ATM for the IRS.

Corner 3
Opportunity Planning

My legacy is made manifest in my children, just as I carry my father's, and so on. If my children merely echo me, then I have failed. My purpose in life—my legacy—is to lift them to the next level.

Edsel Ford III

T OO OFTEN, CERTAIN ASPECTS OF ESTATE PLANNING ARE PERCEIVED as a stick, not a carrot. As in "He's out of my will if he doesn't stop drinking!" In our experience, pronouncements like that rarely inspire anything but resentment. True inspiration, the kind that energizes people, is the realm of Corner Three in the Four Corners plan: opportunity planning.

Conversations about renegade family members and "protection-from" topics can blunt anybody's excitement. Changing the subject to opportunities is a sure-fire way to get the conversation flowing again. In fact, it's like opening the floodgates to a reservoir of ideas, just waiting for a chance to pour out.

As we've said often, a legacy is a living and growing thing. It's not a set of rules or even rewards. A legacy evolves over the generations, propelled by both your values and what your heirs *do* with your values. Will they experience them as guardrails or launching pads? When you've left a legacy that encourages, supports, and rewards, you're building a platform of opportunities underneath the generations and inviting them to soar.

Imagine two discussions. The first: "I'd like to give you a portion of my wealth so that you have opportunities I didn't." And the second: "These are the kinds of things that have shaped me, and made my life fulfilling—my years in the Boy Scouts, building a business that made a difference in people's lives, and the deepening relationships of family. How about you? What does a fulfilling life look like to you?" Guess where the richest conversations occur.

A legacy brought to life by creating opportunity isn't measured in dollars. No matter how large or how modest your estate, you can build a plan that helps set your heirs on courses that will honor your legacy and embody their own values. Let's look at some of the best ways and best ideas we've seen.

ENCOURAGE POSITIVE CHOICES AND OPTIMAL RESULTS

For most of us, wealth is difficult to amass. It takes hard work and sacrifice, often for decades. Along the way we dig a well of self-knowledge that's there for us to draw upon at least as often as we draw on any financial account. In your mind, you'd probably be hard pressed to separate the money from the lessons learned while generating it—they're both valuable. For many years, estate plans only provided a pathway for passing money. The life lessons that can't be measured in dollars simply didn't fit in the planning tools of the day. Untold millions have been squandered by heirs with too much money and not enough...well, pick it... discipline, wisdom, perspective, kindness, humility, self-control, ambition, hunger, or patience.

There's a phrase we hear a lot: "from shirtsleeves to shirt-sleeves in four generations." The idea inside the words is equal parts resignation and warning: From humble beginnings, the first generation builds the fortune while preserving their values, even their wardrobe. The second generation takes the opportunities their parents have created for them and moves to the city, joins the museum board, and upgrades their wardrobe while the fortune plateaus. Generation three knows only comfort and nice clothes and tears into the fortune to satisfy their appetites. The fourth generation has no choice but to put on a work shirt and start earning it again. Simplistic? Of course, but there are versions of it in Italian, Spanish, Gaelic, and even Chinese cultures, which must say something about the universal human difficulties in transferring wealth past one generation.

In an 1891 essay with the provocative title of *The Advantages of Poverty*, the industrialist Andrew Carnegie wrote that "the parent who leaves his son enormous wealth generally deadens the talents and energies of the son, and tempts him to lead a less useful and less worthy life than he otherwise would." Overlooking Mr. Carnegie's apparent assumption that daughters had no use for talents and energies, we can sympathize with his frustrations. Warren Buffett has them too, saying famously in *Fortune* magazine that "the perfect amount to leave to [one's] children is 'enough money so that they would feel they could do anything, but not so much that they could do nothing.'" Now there's an implied question, and for many people the answers are found in incentive trusts.

Incentive trusts

In its basic form, an incentive trust requires the beneficiary to meet certain milestones that you define when establishing the trust. When the milestones are reached, beneficiaries receive distributions of income and principal, which are also defined in advance. This is the carrot approach to passing wealth and, hope-fully, values. Of course, values aren't passed as much as they are modeled by you. After all, are your core values exactly the same as your parents'? They probably share much of the same territory, but also undoubtedly reflect your own life experiences. You lived your way into your values and incentive trusts can give your heirs the opportunity to do the same. A few examples:

Encourage entrepreneurship: If building a business is part of your story, you can give your heirs the chance to build theirs by making trust assets available to launch a business.

Encourage employment: If you believe that work is vital to building self-worth and self-sufficiency, then you can have the trust match a beneficiary's earned income with distributions in a specified amount or percentage.

Encourage savings and prudent investing: Frugality and astute investing are at the core of many people's financial suc-cess. Those values and practices can be rewarded by distributions when the beneficiary's personal assets reach a certain amount.

Encourage service as a career: For the children and grand-children of many clients, accumulating wealth may take a back-seat to serving people as teachers, clergy, or social workers. Those are ennobling choices that don't have to be impoverishing.

Encourage a family focus: Stay-at-home parents can sacri-fice income for their children. It's a difficult choice that can be made easier by providing income replacement to a beneficiary who leaves the workplace to raise a family or who chooses to stay home and raise the kids instead of establishing a career.

Encourage academic success: Often times, the foundation of our values is established by the academic rigors of college and the confidence generated by success in this setting. An incentive trust can tie distributions directly to performance in school— either graduation or a specific GPA.

Encourage victories large and small: Incentive trusts can provide matching funds to scholarships earned, distributions when an heir attains an Eagle Scout designation, even maintaining a good driving record.

Encourage sobriety: Substance abuse and addiction is an all-too-common problem among the children and grandchildren of affluent families. An incentive trust can tie distributions to completion of a substance abuse treatment program and add provisions for ongoing distributions contingent upon staying clean and sober.

Scout's Honor

No matter how large our fortune, we don't look back on our life and think of it as the mere accumulation of wealth. It's relationships and experiences that we value, as we appreciate how each contributed to our success. Very often my clients want to make experiences possible for their children or grandchildren. It could be a semester studying abroad or something of a larger scale, like the opportunity to choose a career based on passion rather than income-earning potential. My clients have often chosen to plan their estates to provide motivation or opportunities that they feel will make their family members "better people" rather than "rich kids."

(continued)

One client explained that his childhood was shaped by his involvement in the Boy Scouts and that he hoped that his grandchildren would share the same or similar experiences. For that particular client, we wrote trust provisions that would provide incentives for the parents to have their children participate in scouting by providing that all expenses associated with such participation would be paid by the trust. As additional incentive for the grandchildren to fully participate, the trust provided a payment of $1,000 to any grandchild who achieved the rank of Eagle Scout or its equivalent.

I've written trusts that are set up with a dollar match provision that encourages employment, especially in the not-for-profit sector. If the child goes to work in a for-profit business, the trust distributes a 50 percent match up to a certain dollar limit. If the child goes to work for a not-for-profit organization, the distributions shift up to a 100 percent dollar match. This novel structure "evens the playing field" to some degree, allowing the young person to make a career decision based on where their heart is pointing them.

Brad Galbraith

Remember that with plans, as with cars, "your mileage may vary." At best, we make educated guesses about the future. Hopes can be dashed in a moment; unexpected encounters can send us in completely new directions. As John Lennon quipped, "Life is what happens while you're busy making other plans." So, too, your plans for your heirs, which means there are a few elements that round out every incentive trust in a Four Corners plan.

Communicate: It's absolutely essential that you communicate the objectives of the trust and your hopes for what it can mean to your heirs. For some, it helps to craft a mission statement that ties together your intent for the full set of incentives. This document should also address the level of flexibility granted to the trustee. The key is transparency—formally and informally make your wishes known and your reasons clear. As we wrote earlier in this chapter, opportunities inspire the best kinds of family discussions.

Specificity: Use language that is crystal clear—"a 3.5 GPA on a 4.0 scale" is better than "good grades." If distributions are to be based upon earned income, the trust must define "earned income" in detail. For example, self-employed individuals have different measuring sticks for income. Verification should specify tax returns from accountants, transcripts from bursars and, as uncomfortable as it may be to include, drug test results from certified labs.

Flexibility: How can you be specific *and* flexible? It begins by identifying the right trustee and then empowering them with discretion to interpret the circumstances that the trust hasn't anticipated. If the beneficiary becomes disabled and is no longer able to work, will the trustee be authorized to, for example, purchase a wheelchair-equipped van? This is a vital role—more than a gatekeeper, they're also a judge. Pick one with the guts to say no and the courage to say yes. Then, just to balance that power, we highly recommend naming a trust protector for every incentive trust.

If you're reading this and saying, "Well that sounds complicated," you're right. Incentive trusts are a more complex strategy than basic trusts that distribute automatically at death or when beneficiaries reach certain ages. But no matter how complex or simple your planning, your estate will pass from your cup to their cups. Integrating what you've learned and experienced into incentive trusts, you can help your heirs fill a cup and keep it all from spilling out.

Family banks

Incentive trusts give your plan a degree of precision: Here's the incentive and here's the reward. A family bank is similar in that it makes trust assets available to your heirs as they mature, but it's less specific in what those behaviors are and the dollar amounts they distribute. A family bank isn't an actual bank, but it can function in much the same way a traditional bank does. It loans money to help new ventures get started and to help existing companies grow. It can help newlyweds begin life together in a home and it can grow its own assets to help fund opportunities for generations of heirs.

Unlike an incentive trust, a family bank doesn't promise to reward an accomplishment; it's a financial boost when needed that comes with a very real-world requirement: The money is to be paid back.

A family bank is simply a dynasty trust (explained in the Protection Planning chapter) combined with an LLC. It's funded by periodic or annual gifts or by a distribution at death and then kept flush by repayments and interest accrued. The loans are typically at a below-market interest rate and have substantially lower underwriting thresholds. That doesn't mean the money is handed out without merit because that's the role of its administrator.

The trustee selects an administrator, someone independent to the family and typically with experience in banking or business investing. The administrator then evaluates the opportunities on the same criteria a bank would, i.e., the purpose for the loan, the creditworthiness of the borrower, etc.

Repayment terms are established and the family bank makes the loan.

The bank is established with a set of provisions, including what percentage of the assets can be loaned to any family member at one time, how the trust funds are invested when not out on loan, the process for overruling the administrator by the trustee, and the security interest that the bank takes in case the loan can't be repaid.

We've seen family banks at the center of thriving families; they can provide the financing for home ownership and business growth. One family bank even makes money available for large family vacations. And when they are adequately funded, soundly structured, and prudently managed, a family bank can endure for generations, giving successive groups of heirs the chance to construct their expression of your legacy.

FUND EDUCATION AND HEALTH CARE EXPENSES

In Chapter 2, we explored how gifts keep estate assets inside the family while taking them outside the taxable estate. Those are gifts directly to family members and count against the AGE, or annual gift exclusion. There's another way to gift that generates opportunities for your heirs and doesn't eat up your AGE, and it all comes down to that one line on the check: payable to _____.

It's a delight when we can tell clients they can write a check to their kid's or grandkid's school and not add a penny to the gifting total that matters to the IRS. "We can do that?" Yep. When you pay the school directly, your heir isn't receiving the money, so it's not, technically, a gift. But what a gift it is when you can fund, or partially fund, an education for your heirs. There's even more good news for those clients: Health care expenses paid don't count against your exclusion either.

You can write a check to a health care provider and not impact your AGE and not just acute care delivered in a hospital setting either. How about Lasik surgery? How about cosmetic or reconstructive surgery? Even bariatric surgery can be paid for directly without impacting your gifting totals. Some may roll their eyes here, but for many people their opportunities in life are intricately tied to their physical appearance. Removing a birthmark may mean renewed confidence in an interview. A once obese person is now carrying an appropriate weight and can participate in life more fully. When the health care purchased is closer to the acute side of the spectrum, it's impossible to calculate the kinds of opportunities you are making possible. Ask anyone who has recovered from a serious illness; their health is a springboard to a richer, more satisfying life.

Section 529 plans are qualified tuition programs that have roared into the educational planning world. For good reason, too, because earnings on your contributions to a 529 plan are exempt from federal and state income tax while the funds remain in the plan account. In many states you may also qualify for an income tax deduction for a portion of your contribution, depending on your income. What's more, 529 *distributions* are also exempt from federal and state income tax if the distribution is used for the qualified higher education expenses of the child or grandchild. That includes not only tuition, room, board, fees, books, and supplies, but also computers and other equipment.

Those are mostly well-understood advantages of a 529. What often surprises clients is that contributions to a 529 can be pre-paid against future AGE limits. In a single year, you can contribute up to five times the $13,000 annual exclusion amount, or $65,000. Your spouse can even contribute a separate $65,000. It's a one-time gift that gives the account a most robust principal balance to build upon. Then, at tax time, the IRS allows for your gifts to be spread over five years. Provided you live at least five years and your gift does not exceed the cumulative exclusion amount, your gift qualifies for the gift tax annual exclusion. If the gift is for grandchildren, the benefits are multiplied since the gift will be excluded from the generation-skipping transfer tax as well.

MULTIPLY OPPORTUNITIES WITH CHARITABLE TRUST PLANNING

We're transitioning now into a different zone within Corner Three. Charitable planning is another key component of opportunity planning.

In our offices, conversations around charitable giving are often part of a client's life transition. The kids are grown and prospering. The grandkids are right behind them. The estate planning to date has done the job of protecting the wealth and establishing the trusts to pass it. Now what?

For many, the energy shifts from their role as patriarchs and matriarchs to their passions as human beings. In some circles, it's called philanthropy, which sounds to us like buying your name onto a building. That's a simplistic position to be sure, but philanthropy can become more about the philanthropist than the people he or she is helping. In Four Corners Land, we call it charitable planning and keep the focus on charity in all its dimensions.

The Greeks called it *caritas* and it meant "love for all people." Charity is about the people receiving, not the person giving. It describes our conversations with our clients. "How can we help?" is a better way to talk about opportunities than "What do we get out of it?" (But don't worry; you can get a lot out of it.)

Charities don't want your cash.

Donating after-tax dollars to charity steals a little bit from both you and the charity. You miss out on a larger deduction and the charity misses out on the gains that probably generated the money in the first place. A better alternative to donating cash is highly appreciated assets. When you donate a low basis stock to charity, you receive a charitable income tax deduction equal to the current value of the stock at the date of donation. Then, the charity can sell the stock without paying capital gains tax and you get a deduction based on the full market value of the asset. Lower taxes mean a more robust donation and a stronger charity.

Robert O'Dell

Charitable Remainder Trusts

Charitable Remainder Trusts (CRTs) are some of the most perfect things in estate planning. They can benefit you, your family, and the charitable causes you care most about. You could say that with CRTs, you can have your cake, eat it, and still have plenty to feed the hungry. Even the IRS loves them. In the most basic terms, a CRT is an irrevocable trust that receives gifted property—usually appreciated stock or real estate, but other assets can also be contributed. The donor of the property typically designates himself or herself as trustee and the donor and spouse are typically named as the CRT's income beneficiaries for their lifetimes. The control stays with you, the income goes to you, and when you're gone, any assets left in the CRT are distributed to one or more charities. Beautiful, and this is just the beginning. With a properly crafted CRT you can:

Avoid capital gains tax on highly appreciated stock, a business interest, real estate, or other appreciated assets. The CRT receives the assets and then sells them. All the proceeds remain in the trust, not just what's left after taxes.

Create income by converting highly appreciated, low-yielding assets (or illiquid holdings like real estate) to higher income-producing assets. And that's without first absorbing a capital gains hit.

Build a retirement nest egg from a business or professional practice on a tax-deferred basis while avoiding the limitations of a qualified retirement plan.

Transfer a business to an heir by gifting it to a CRT. The business shares, once transferred to the CRT, can be repurchased by an heir who is a minority shareholder, who can then take control. The grantors also avoid the gift tax, receive a lifetime income, avoid capital gains on the sale of stock, and, depending on age and the payout rates, receive a sizable tax deduction, too.

When the trust is first established, you must select the percentage payout and, once you do, it can't be changed. The percentage selected must be at least 5 percent of the value of the assets in the trust and the actual dollar amount paid to you is usually based on the value of the trust assets as revalued each year. The lower the percentage, the more value stays (and grows) inside the trust. Over time, a lower percentage payout can often produce more total income for you. Then, on the passing of the last income beneficiary, trust assets are distributed to the selected charities. Assuming the CRT is properly structured, there will be no estate tax due.

There are other forms of the CRT that allow for equal annual payments (or no payments) with the potential for a makeup at a future date of the grantor's choice. Four Corners planning helps you determine which choice is right.

And why, exactly, does the IRS love this kind of trust?

The federal government actually encourages the establishment of Charitable Remainder Trusts. Laws governing CRTs reflect Congress's intention to motivate taxpayers' charitable giving. Their logic says a taxpayer's dollar that goes to work for charity saves the government more than a dollar that would ultimately be paid in a benefit of some kind. Charitable Remainder Trusts are efficient. The government? Not so much.

Wealth Replacement Trusts: Replacing Wealth and Restoring Calm

Several of my clients over the years of my practice have seen the wisdom of creating a Charitable Remainder Trust (CRT) to provide substantial benefits for themselves and their families while they are alive, and a charitable legacy at their deaths. The CRT is a truly synergistic estate planning tool. It can provide a way to avoid capital gains taxes on the sale of one or more highly appreciated assets, give you or a loved one a lifetime of income, create a charitable legacy that can last decades, and provide a sizable tax deduction. Everybody wins—everybody but your heirs. In essence, one or more charities will benefit at the expense of your heirs. This is easily solved through the use of a Wealth Replacement Trust (WRT).

A WRT can be set up to replace any portion of the value of the assets contributed to a CRT. It is usually funded with a life insurance policy, paid for from your gifts to the WRT. The source of your gifts could be the tax savings realized from the tax deduction when assets are contributed to the CRT. In addition to the tax savings, a portion of the CRT's periodic distribution can be gifted to the WRT. It is a truly win-win strategy, as the example below illustrates.

The Alberts, ages 65/63, good health, 2 children	Without CRT	With CRT
Market Value of Appreciated Property	$3,000,000	$3,000,000
Gift to Charity, at second death (CRT)	0	$3,000,000 +/-
Capital Gains Tax on sale @ 15% (Basis = 0)	<$450,000>	0
Available to Invest after sale	$2,550,000	$3,000,000
Annual Income from Proceeds @ 7%	$178,500	$210,000
Tax Deduction @ Fed. 7520 Rate of 3%	N/A	$640,000
Tax Savings from Deduction @ 35%	N/A	$224,000
Insurance (paid from tax savings + $24,000/year)	N/A	$3,000,000
Gross Estate to Children before Tax	$2,550,000	$3,000,000
Estate Taxes @ 35%	<$892,500>	N/A
Net to Children	$1,657,500	$3,000,000
Net to Charity	N/A	$3,000,000
Total Wealth Transferred	$1,657,500	$6,000,000

With a CRT, Mr. and Mrs. Albert will enjoy a higher income during their lives. Their two children will end up with a much larger inheritance, and a charity, in this case the Albert Family Foundation, will have enough to truly make a difference—keeping the Albert name and legacy alive for a very long time.

Mike Kilbourn

Wealth Replacement Trusts

It's a rare client who makes charitable planning a larger priority than their family. And yet, heirs can see the wealth designated for charity as wealth they won't inherit. It's true, they won't. Now maybe you can ease their worries by appealing to their charitable nature. Or maybe not, in which case a Wealth Replacement Trust (WRT) can return some calm to the conversation.

A WRT is an irrevocable trust created exclusively to benefit your heirs. It is funded with the taxes saved by the CRT's income tax deductions, plus a portion of the cash flow generated from the CRT. Typically the funds are used to purchase life insurance. That policy replaces the value of the gifted assets and, in many cases, generates a larger tax-free inheritance than your heirs would otherwise receive if the transferred assets had remained in your estate. With life insurance in a properly structured WRT, your heirs not only avoid gift and estate taxes, there will be no income taxes as well. That should make everyone happy, including you. (See the sidebar titled "Wealth Replacement Trusts: Replacing Wealth and Restoring Calm" beginning on page 58 for more on wealth replacement trusts.)

Charitable Lead Trusts

Charitable Remainder Trusts have an equally generous opposite called a Charitable Lead Trust (CLT). With it, you can flip-flop the beneficiaries and put charity first (they love that) and your heirs second (they'll love it, too, eventually). In a CLT charities "take the lead" and become the income beneficiaries, receiving a steady stream of income during the life of the trust. When the term of the trust ends, the remaining assets are then transferred to your heirs. Along the way, you receive deductions for the charitable contributions and, if the assets keep appreciating despite the charitable payments, your heirs inherit even more, tax-free.

Just as with CRTs, CLTs must either be an annuity trust or a unitrust. In the case of the charitable lead annuity trust, the annuity is expressed as a percentage of the initial fair market value of the assets contributed to the trust. With a unitrust the annual distribution is calculated each year based on the current value of the trust's assets.

Charitable lead trusts are established and managed while you are alive. Some clients would rather save this kind of charitable giving until after their death. Enter the Testamentary Charitable Lead Trust. It's built while you're alive and goes into effect at the time of your death. Income is paid to the charity for a pre-set period of time, after which the trust assets are distributed to your heirs. We've heard these kinds of trusts called "wait awhile trusts." The principal of the trust is still in the family, but they'll have to wait a while before receiving it. It's a great way to reduce estate taxes at your passing, while you're doing good for charity *and* your family.

CRTs come in assorted shades of smart.

If you can stand a quick detour into estate planning's jungle of acronyms, follow us into the CRUTs, NIMCRUTs, and CRATs.

A CRUT is a Charitable Remainder Unitrust. It gives you the ability to add contributions to the trust at any time, which means the total value of the trust assets is going to change over time. Because CRUT payments are based on a percentage of trust assets, they pay a variable distribution amount. Each year, the current value of the trust is determined and then multiplied by the payout rate to calculate the current year's distribution.

A CRUT can also be set up as a Net Income Charitable Remainder Unitrust, or NIMCRUT. That handsomely

(continued)

named trust contains a special provision that allows the trustee to hold for future sale or invest the sale proceeds into non-income-producing investments such as zero-coupon bonds, deferred annuities, growth securities, or raw land. The trust specifies that the trustee should only distribute the trust's "net income." But since the assets mentioned above do not usually produce income, there would be no "net income" and no annual payout. Instead, the trustee creates a "make-up" account for the amounts that remain unpaid each period. This make-up account accumulates until the trustee decides to shift the investment portfolio to income-producing assets. Then, if the income from the capital gains and from the new investments exceeds the chosen percentage payout for a given period, the beneficiary receives the additional income. Yep, CRUTs are complex, that's why CRATs were created.

A CRAT, or Charitable Remainder Annuity Trust, lets you make a one-time contribution and then pays distributions at a fixed rate. Like all CRTs, the fixed payout can't be less than 5 percent of the initial amount contributed and there is no need to revalue the assets annually. If the income of the CRAT is less than the mandatory annual payout, the balance of the distribution is taken from principal.

GUIDE HEIRS TOWARD RESPONSIBLE CITIZENSHIP

We've left out something important in the discussions above about charitable strategies: the charities. Assets or income from the trusts discussed above can be used to benefit specific organizations, like a church, school, or museum. Assets can be directed to community organizations like the United Way or the many other community development organizations working to improve life in the places they call home. No news there, right?

Some people are delighted to discover that trust assets meant for charitable use don't even have to leave the family's control. Assets generated by charitable trusts can flow into a Private Family Foundation (if you've established one) or into a Donor Advised Fund. (See the following sidebar titled "Involvement and Impact: Donor Advised Funds and Private Family Foundations" for more about both of these options.) In the Four Corners plan there's room for both, but we also like to make room at the table for the next generation. Call it "legacy training."

We advise charitably minded clients to see their financial gifts as both charity and education. By handing your heirs some (or all) responsibility for managing the foundation's assets and determining which charities should benefit, you put them in a great position to make a difference while they strengthen their leadership and decision-making skills. They see what financial administration and investment strategies look like from the inside. And the most lasting lessons may come from getting close to the organizations working hard to improve lives and to the people whose lives are better because of *your* wealth and *their* decisions. Vital and generative legacies are born in these moments.

Involvement and Impact: Donor Advised Funds and Private Family Foundations

Donor Advised Funds are a subaccount of a public charitable organization. They're the sponsor and you can set up your own account with them, often at no cost. You can donate assets to your account, receive a charitable deduction, avoid capital gain taxes, and advise the fund as to which charitable organizations should receive their distributions. At its core, it's an elegant structure, but not all funds are equal.

(continued)

There are primarily four types of fund sponsors:

• Local community foundations
• Large national charitable organizations
• Investment companies
• Independent national community foundations

Local community foundations often have geographic restrictions on where grants can be made and can require the assets in your account to become a part of the general fund after two or three generations. Large national charitable organizations often restrict grants to charitable organizations that share the same religious or social ideology. And investment firms that offer donor advised funds may restrict the donor on the investment. An independent national fund may give you flexibility that you might not have with other sponsors.

Through your donor advised fund, you can typically make grants to any 501(c)(3) charitable organization throughout the U.S. There may be some restrictions, so be sure you understand the flexibility allowed.

How about Private Family Foundations? They can work well for families with an inclination to stay active and involved in the foundation's business. Family foundations are more common in ultra wealthy families because they do require a significant financial investment to establish and administer, but assets really aren't the primary determinant. Family foundations are great options when the primary desire is to involve family members. I've seen families with relatively modest estates hop gladly through the administration hoops in order to give their family members a meaningful role in evaluating charitable organizations and distributing dollars.

Robert O'Dell

TALK YOUR WAY TO A LEGACY THAT ENDURES

With everything that makes the Opportunity Planning corner so dynamic, the real energy inside it isn't wealth; it's understanding. Understanding is the by-product of many things, including conversation, candor, patience, and trust. When your family understands the true dimension of the legacy you've imagined, good things follow. Conversely, your understanding must make room for your heirs to pilot their own lives. The most important thing you can offer them is not a precise flight plan, but a GPS. In the closing chapter you'll encounter some of the tools and ideas that can bring understanding to life in your family. In the practice of building a Four Corners plan, we return again and again to the importance of a dialogue among the family, *about* the family. It's not always convenient or comfortable. Yet, getting out of your comfort zone and inviting others to meet you there is where meaningful opportunities can take root.

A Charitable Policy: Using Life Insurance as a Giving Strategy

Some time ago, I decided to create a scholarship fund for qualified, motivated students who need financial help at the university where I did most of my undergraduate and graduate studies. I didn't just write a check though; I leveraged the advantages of life insurance.

I considered gifting an existing policy, which would have provided an immediate tax deduction for the value of the policy—a figure close to the total premiums paid. However, I elected to purchase a new policy, the premiums of which were a fraction of the actual benefit that will fund

(continued)

the scholarship program I designed with the help of the university's Development Director. My annual premium checks were deductible because I made my checks payable to the university, which applied them to the policy premiums. After several years, the policy built up enough cash value to sustain the death benefit, so I was able to discontinue making gifts to cover the premiums.

In the future, if the policy requires additional premiums to sustain the death benefit, I can elect to make more gifts or the university can make them from their existing funds. Alternatively, the university, with my cooperation, could elect to sell that policy in what is known as a "life settlement" transaction for more than the current cash value—some percentage of the death benefit. This would produce less benefit to my scholarship fund, but has the added benefit of putting the fund in place while I'm alive.

Mike Kilbourn

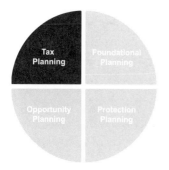

Corner 4
Tax Planning

Inheritance taxes are so high that the happiest mourner at a rich man's funeral is usually Uncle Sam.

Olin Miller

YOU'VE BEEN TRICKED.

It's the same kind of trick you used to pull on your kids, or maybe still do on your grandkids: They think they're eating a yummy bowl of pasta, and they are, but you also sneaked in a bunch of veggies by dicing them up and mixing it all up in the sauce. Taxes are the veggies. Everything else is the sauce.

While you've arrived at the Tax Planning corner, we've actually been talking taxes all along. Nearly every Four Corners trust and strategy you've read about so far offers meaningful tax advantages. These trusts and strategies either help reduce taxes on your estate or sidestep them altogether. But we get it; reading about taxes can be about as much fun as paying them. So we sneaked them in, especially in Corners Two and Three, "Protection Planning" and "Opportunity Planning." However, if you're the kind of reader who loves tax-talk and always keeps a calculator nearby, we have some things for you to dig into. In this chapter, we'll highlight some of the tax advantages within approaches you've already read about and introduce you to several strategies that are 100 percent pure tax planning.

We're all familiar with Ben Franklin's quip about the certainty of just two things: death and taxes. In the estate planning business, they pretty much overlap. In fact, to many of our clients there's little difference at all—"When I die, the taxes will kill what's left." It's this perception—right or wrong—that most often compels people to begin their estate planning in earnest. We all wish there was more we could do about death; but taxes don't have to loom quite so inevitably.

Taxes and the Non-Citizen Spouse

In my practice, one of the first questions I ask married couples is whether they are U.S. citizens. The answer to this crucial question will have a major impact on the couple's planning. Not only do transfers between spouses become subject to gift taxes, but also, if one spouse is a U.S. citizen and the other is not, care must be taken to draft "qualified domestic trust" (QDOT) provisions. Absent compliance with these technical tax code requirements, non-citizen spouses cannot inherit even modest sums without suffering substantial estate taxation. This is because only U.S. citizen spouses are entitled to the unlimited marital deduction.

By properly planning the estate to comply with QDOT requirements, a non-citizen spouse will only be subject to taxation when the funds are withdrawn from the QDOT. The opportunity to defer taxation is not nearly as beneficial to a surviving non-citizen spouse as the unlimited marital deduction; yet, for substantial estates, the financial impact is similar. For more modest estates, the difference between tax deferral and the unlimited marital deduction is very substantial—so substantial, in fact, that some of the best advice I can give to a non-citizen spouse in that situation is to start working on becoming a U.S. citizen.

Fortunately, if the U.S. citizen spouse dies and the surviving spouse later becomes a U.S. citizen, the QDOT requirements will then terminate and the unlimited marital deduction will spring back to life.

Brad Galbraith

CONSIDER THE PARADOX OF TAX PLANNING

In our modern world, planning appears to be the very definition of a forward-looking act. However the word "plan" is not rooted in the abstractions of preparing for some future event, but in the very physical act of building. The Latin *planum* translates as "a flat or level surface." It was used to describe the starting point for building a structure. "Before you start, level the ground." Makes sense, of course, and not just for carpenters.

Estate planning looks forward, too, and working with our clients, we build a plan that anticipates life's future events, including its ending. The level ground we begin with is current tax laws and assorted regulations. Unfortunately, it's also like building your house right on top of an earthquake fault line—the level ground underneath estate planning is almost always gradually shifting; sporadically, it even shudders and shakes. In other words, planning happens on the legal and political ground of the moment and that ground is almost certain to change, putting the plan itself at risk of failing to deliver.

Estate planners live in this paradox: We craft plans that would succeed if our client got hit by a bus 20 minutes after signing the documents, but they probably won't get hit by anything for years or even decades into the future when that plan becomes a building. Will it be strong enough?

Throughout this book we've explored mechanisms that can give plans the flexibility they need to accommodate life's little earthquakes. Life *is* change and good planning accommodates it. Tax laws on the other hand are a lot less predictable than growing up and growing old. They move on an unseen surface of regulatory bulletins and legal rulings; they shake on the legislative maneuverings and political ideology of the party in power. Tax rates, annual limits, even estate taxes themselves are not biblical laws; they can be rewritten and inevitably will be.

The Roth IRA: To Convert or Not Convert

With a traditional IRA, contributions are tax deductible but withdrawals are taxable income. With a Roth IRA, contributions generate no deductions, but the withdrawals are tax-free. Which one is right for you? It's an important decision, but not always a decision you'll have to live with until you retire.

In 2006, Congress passed the Pension Protection Act, which allows for individuals, regardless of income, to convert their traditional (rollover) IRAs to Roth IRAs beginning in 2010. After the conversion, the Roth IRA owner must defer withdrawals for a minimum of five years in order to receive tax-free income.

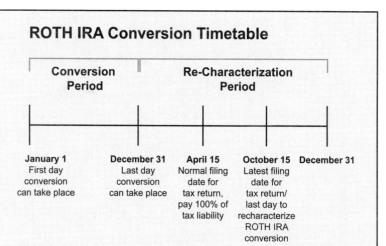

ROTH IRA Conversion Timetable

Conversion Period		Re-Characterization Period		
January 1 First day conversion can take place	**December 31** Last day conversion can take place	**April 15** Normal filing date for tax return, pay 100% of tax liability	**October 15** Latest filing date for tax return/ last day to recharacterize ROTH IRA conversion	**December 31**

Mulligan Rule: Roth IRA rules offer new convertees a "free-look," during which they can change back to a traditional pre-tax IRA for any reason and have their tax liability for the Roth conversion eliminated. The recharacterization must take place no later than October 15th of the year after conversion. The most likely reasons for recharacterizations would be poor investment performance or unanticipated tax consequences (see Roth IRA Conversion Timetable).

While the Mulligan Rule helps answer the question of whether to convert or not, we recommend converting at the beginning of the calendar year. However, the Mulligan Rule raises a new question: "Do you keep the newly converted Roth IRA or recharactherize it back to a traditional IRA?" The answer to that question is solved by the investment performance during the free look period.

No Cherry Picking: The IRS does not allow partial Roth IRA recharacterizations. The IRA owner must

(continued)

decide if they wish to keep the Roth IRA and pay taxes on the converted amount or send it all back to the traditional IRA. So if you have two investments in your Roth IRA, and one performs very well and the other not as well, you are not permitted to keep the winner and send back the loser.

Another strategy: Segregated Roths: A proven approach to ensure Roth conversion success is to have multiple Roth IRA accounts. Each account would have a separate and non-correlated investment strategy; if one account performs very well and the other account performs not as well, you can send back the Roth IRA that did not do as well and keep the best performing account.

Segregated Accounts

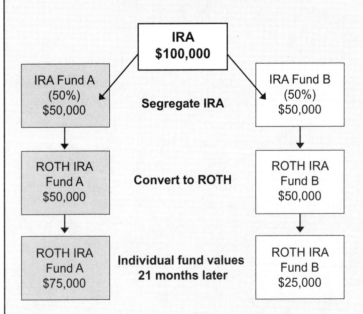

You can keep Fund A and recharacterize Fund B

Robert O'Dell

KNOW YOUR OPPONENTS—THE TAX COLLECTORS

There are two groups of tax collectors to keep in mind as you plan. The first is the most fearsome, the IRS. Federal officials collect estate tax, income tax, and capital gains tax, and they monitor your gift giving to calculate your gift tax. For most people, these taxes represent the greatest threat and the best reason for comprehensive estate planning. They are not, however, the only taxes you may face.

At a state level, there are additional hazards, some with the same name: income, estate, and capital gains. Depending on your state of residence, you may be exposed to a state income tax, state estate taxes, or state inheritance taxes. And where exactly is your state of residence? The answer may be more complicated than you think; it's certainly more important to get it right if you have homes in two or more states. Those are domicile issues and later in this chapter Mike Kilbourn gives you a quick tour.

Which brings us to a big asterisk: Talk to your advisor. These strategies and scenarios are general guidelines and illustrations. They're not specific advice. The Four Corners website, www.fourcornersplan.com, was also updated with new laws and rates after this edition was printed. As you read, you'll see the areas that are ripe for an online refresh.

Using a Stretch IRA

The Stretch IRA is a wealth transfer method that allows an IRA owner to "stretch" their IRA distributions over future generations, providing the maximum benefit possible. When the IRA owner reaches age 70½, he or she is required to take required minimum distributions

(continued)

(RMDs) which are calculated via a special IRS table. If you are fortunate enough to inherit someone else's IRA, you will be required to take RMDs each year from the inherited IRA account based on your remaining life expectancy. IRAs allow the owner or beneficiary to take any amount from an IRA at any time. Assuming no taxes were ever paid on the IRA contributions, the withdrawals will be taxable. So leaving as much as possible in an IRA to continue to grow tax deferred is usually the best course of action.

To stretch out the time over which withdrawals may be taken and provide the optimum payout over time, only the RMDs should be withdrawn. The result of this strategy can be dramatic. For example, Patrick, age 65, has a $1 million traditional IRA. He wants to maximize cumulative withdrawals for himself, his wife Mary, age 62, and his three children. Using the stretch strategy, taking only the RMDs, here are the results:

ASSUMPTIONS:

- 6% compounded earnings rate
- Patrick, age 65, lives 15 more years and dies at age 80
- Patrick starts his withdrawals the year he turns 70½, taking only the RMDs
- Mary converts Patrick's IRA to her own at his death and takes only the RMDs
- Mary lives 7 additional years and dies at age 85

RESULTS:

- Patrick withdraws only the RMDs, which total **$720,918**

- The balance in Patrick's IRA at his death is $1,589,979

- Mary withdraws only the RMDs totaling **$665,527**

- The balance at Mary's death is $1,601,716

- The IRA balance of $1,601,716 is divided into three accounts of $533,905 for the children

- Pat, Jr., age 63, withdraws RMDs based on his 22-year life expectancy;

  total withdrawals = **$1,169,173**

- Mike, age 58, withdraws RMDs based on his 27-year life expectancy;

  total withdrawals = **$1,368,932**

- Barb, age 53, withdraws RMDs based on her 32-year life expectancy;

  total withdrawals = **$1,618,706**

The total received by Patrick, Mary, Pat, Jr., Mike, and Barb over the 55 years equals **$5,543,256**. Comparing this to the $1 million in Patrick's IRA at age 65 clearly demonstrates the power of the Stretch IRA strategy.

If income needs are not an issue for your spouse and children, then naming younger beneficiaries, such as grandchildren or great-grandchildren, can allow you to stretch the value of your IRA over additional generations.

Mike Kilbourn

DEVELOP A GIFT STRATEGY TO MANEUVER THROUGH THE GIFT MINEFIELD

On the Protection Planning corner, we explored how gifts can be used to keep wealth under the family tree. To recap: Outright gifts are just like they sound—you give them with no strings attached; custodial accounts are gifts that arrive when your heirs reach predetermined age milestones; and Crummey trusts give you a place to park future gift dollars outside of the estate. In that chapter we also warned against triggering gift taxes by exceeding annual or lifetime limits. But what, exactly, are gift taxes? And more pointedly, can you gift your way into a big tax bill even as you lower your estate's taxable value?

Gift taxes are not like sales tax, capital gain, or income tax in that they are due at, or relatively close to, the transaction. Those taxes may grind down your capitalist enthusiasm, but at least you can see them coming and get them behind you quickly. Not gift taxes. These taxes are not immediately due; they're just immediately *filed*. Annually, the IRS wants to be notified as to each gift, who received it, and how much. That information accumulates year after year in the IRS file with your name on it. If you exceed the AGE, or Annual Gift Exclusion ($13,000 as of this printing), your file reflects that in year X you over-gifted by Y. Those Y dollars are logged annually and then totaled once you pass away. That's the amount that the revenuers return to your taxable estate, even though the dollars themselves may have been gone for years. Taxation without denomination, if you will. And it doesn't stop there.

As we also touched on the Protection Planning corner, you have another gift ceiling that you can work up to. It's the Lifetime Exclusion and it's a completely separate accounting from your AGE. The exclusion amount as of this printing was $5 million per person. These are the major gifts meant to clear five and six digit amounts from your taxable estate. If you have the wealth and the family to hand it off to, it's a rapid reduction strategy for your estate taxes. The downside is the donor's cost basis transfers to the donee, which means when the donee sells the appreciated asset, it generates capital gains. It won't be your problem, but it's also important to make sure your heirs are fully aware of the hazard and are well advised in how to minimize capital gain taxes or avoid them altogether.

A final thought on gifts: Hitting your gift limits doesn't limit all gifting options. There's no dollar ceiling on how much you can pay to fund an education or cover medical bills. As long as you pay the school or the health care provider directly, the IRS doesn't classify it as a gift. If you're simply looking to drain dollars from your estate and have an heir who needs the help, write that check and take your money out of the revenuers' hands.

SERTs: Keeping the IRS Away without Locking Out Your Spouse

It is a surprise to many of my clients to find out that they can remove assets from their taxable estates and still have indirect access to the income and principal of those assets. A properly drafted Spousal Estate Reduction Trust (SERT) allows you to use your annual gift tax exclusion (currently $13,000 per recipient) and/or part or all of your lifetime gift tax exemption for the benefit of your family, including your spouse. In fact, a spouse may have access to the assets in the SERT for "health, education, maintenance, and support," which covers almost everything.

Indirectly, your spouse may share these assets with you. Besides having access (through your spouse) to trust assets, the SERT allows the growth on the trust assets to escape any

(continued)

gift or estate taxes during your lives. Depending on how long you live, this could save your family a significant amount of tax. The SERT may also contain generation skipping language and allow you to leverage any unused portion of your generation skipping tax exemption. This means that whatever remains in trust at the death of your children can continue in trust for subsequent generations—up to 360 years in Florida—without gift or estate tax at each generation.

Once a SERT is established, I recommend it be funded with assets that have a high basis, as the trust will use that basis for income tax purposes, if and when the asset is sold. I also recommend that the SERT be set up as a "grantor trust" so that all income generated by the trust is taxed to you, as grantor, just as it is currently. This provides an additional benefit—if the income taxes are paid using cash from outside the trust, it allows the trust assets to grow more rapidly. The IRS has ruled favorably on the issue of income taxes paid by the grantor in connection with a grantor trust and concluded that the tax payments do not constitute a gift for gift tax purposes. So paying the income tax for such a trust is a great way to leverage the value of your gifts.

As the trustee and an income beneficiary of the SERT, your spouse should not make gifts to the trust. You, as grantor, must make the gifts and should, if possible, utilize your annual and lifetime gift tax exemptions. Besides having access to trust assets, your spouse, as trustee, typically would be allowed to make distributions from the SERT to other named beneficiaries as their individual needs and circumstances dictate.

If you are married and have hesitated to make gifts because you and your spouse may need access to those assets in the future, why not use the SERT strategy designed in a way that will give you maximum flexibility and provide benefits for several generations of your family?

Mike Kilbourn

STRATEGIZE WITH LIFE INSURANCE

Life insurance is wrapped inside several strategies across the Four Corners. After all, a life insurance policy is one of the smartest ways to reduce estate taxes or to generate the dollars needed to pay them. Along the way, insurance delivers all kinds of meaningful tax advantages—the cash value in permanent life policies accumulates free of current federal, state, and local taxes and the death benefit is paid with no income taxes due.

One of the big cautions with life insurance is keeping the value outside your estate because if you own the policy, it will be part of your gross estate and subject to estate taxes. The counter strategy is to create an irrevocable life insurance trust and make it the policy owner. That's called an ILIT and it's explored more fully in the Protection Planning chapter. If life insurance already figures significantly in your planning to date, make sure you circle back to that corner.

Domicile: More than a Number on the Mailbox

Although the terms "residence" and "domicile" are frequently used as if they have the same meaning, they are not synonymous. A person can have more than one residence in more than one state, but can have only one domicile.

(continued)

Domicile is a person's legal home—his true, fixed
and permanent home and principal establishment, and
to which, whenever he is absent, he has the intention of
returning. This distinction is important, especially when it
comes to state taxes (i.e., income, gift, estate, inheritance,
and intangible taxes). For example, if you are changing
your domicile to a state like Florida, where there are no
such taxes, from a high tax state like New York or Massa-
chusetts, you must take the right steps.

In our book, *The Florida Domicile Handbook* (Brendan
Kelly Publishing, Inc., 2011), Brad Galbraith and I cover
the steps necessary to avoid having the taxing authorities
from your former state breathing down your neck for back
income taxes. As New York Yankees' captain Derek Jeter
learned, you cannot take your domicile change lightly.
New York wanted back taxes of seven figures during a time
when Jeter claimed Florida as his domicile. After costly
attorney fees and lengthy negotiations, Jeter settled with
New York for an unspecified amount and subsequently
took action to properly establish himself as a permanent
Florida resident.

In addition to income tax issues is the problem of
having more than one state looking for state estate or inheritance taxes after you are gone. You won't be around
to fight it; your heirs will! That's what happened to the
heirs of Dr. John Thompson Dorrance, the founder of the
Campbell Soup Company, when he died without clearly
establishing a true, fixed and permanent home. The states
of New Jersey and Pennsylvania ended up collecting approximately $17 million each in state estate taxes at his
death. And the U.S. Supreme Court would not help; in

that case and others, the Court has consistently refused to step in and settle disputes between states in connection with domicile claims. So the burden of proof is on you to properly and effectively establish domicile.

Several steps should be taken to properly establish domicile. Here are a few:

- Spend more time in the chosen state of domicile than in other states where you visit
- Register to vote in your state of domicile
- Obtain a driver's license in your state of domicile
- Title and register your automobile(s) in your state of domicile

You should take change of domicile seriously and minimize your risk of an audit and exposure to attorney fees, taxes, and penalties. Also, taking the proper steps will give you peace of mind knowing you are not exposing your heirs to unexpected claims by multiple states.

Mike Kilbourn

The Four Corners Plan

Connecting the Four Corners

Never say that you know a man until you have divided an inheritance with him.

Johann Kaspar Lavater

Let's circle back to where we began. In the Introduction we invited you to contrast the document-driven transactions that typify conventional estate planning with the higher level dialogues that can generate living legacies. At that stage, the difference between the approaches may have seemed more abstract than meaningful. Our job throughout the tour of the Four Corners has been to define the possibilities of advanced planning in very practical terms—to underline the real difference by expanding your sense of what's possible. Yes, you really can do that.

There *are* ways to craft a legacy that embodies and amplifies what you value most and do it without locking your heirs to a rigid list of rules. If you understand that, we've accomplished much. That doesn't mean, however, that we're finished.

As advanced planning asks more of you, it demands much more of your estate planning attorney and insurance advisors.

Before you enter into these conversations (and well before you write a check), it's absolutely essential to make sure you have the right team working for you. Think about it—building an enduring estate plan is not a simple legal transaction; there's no litigation that delivers a clear verdict. Hard-nosed negotiation and sharp elbows are handy when you need your attorney to be your warrior. Families in conflict are all too common, but estate planning isn't warfare. So then, what *are* the qualities you should look for? We're glad you asked.

THE PRODUCT MENTION

Here's a telling experiment: When you're in an initial conversation with a prospective advisor, see how long it takes for them to mention a specific kind of trust or a financial product. If it happens quickly, it's a troubling sign. Talking product means not listening to people. In our experience, first sessions should be advisors doing just three things: 1) listening, 2) asking clarifying questions, and 3) helping you understand your options. There's no selling. The advisor who rushes to product is the advisor with something to sell. The advisor who listens openly and guides the discussion with open-ended questions is demonstrating what's important to them: you and your visions for your legacy. As we explored earlier, this isn't an interview with crisp, well thought out answers. It's an exploratory conversation. Not feeling it? Explore the exit.

THE STORYTELLER

Stories help people learn. They give facts and figures a heartbeat and invite you to tell a story of your own. We believe estate advisors should tell stories about people, not describe trusts and policies. Estate planning can take you into some deep emotional territory—deeper than what can be reflected in the alphabet soup of trust acronyms. Estate planning advisors should be able to take you there, or meet you there, with more than a legal vocabulary.

THE COLLABORATOR

"Turf" is an ugly word in our business. It means that someone "owns" the relationship (or thinks they do) and works to build a wall around them and you. They don't share recommendations or plans with other advisors, and they don't ask either. Not good. Advanced planning is not about secrets or turf; it's about staying transparent and open. It's about respect for every professional on your team and each of them playing their position when circumstances call for it.

THE SPECIALIST

There's a frenzied consolidation going on in the legal business. Big firms are buying out little firms; big firms are merging with other big firms so they can be, well, bigger. Given the low-growth business climate of the day, there's a business logic to the consolidation. We're not critiquing the firms who make these moves; we are warning you to be skeptical of big firms that use one part of their business to feed new clients into another. Just because your attorney does a good job with your business's contract negotiations doesn't mean his estate planning group is capable of crafting an evolved estate plan. Of course, it's possible, but don't confuse expertise with expedience.

THE COACH

Advanced, values-based estate planning is new territory for most people. Some dance into it with ease, others (OK, most people) need some coaching. An advisor who knows how to coach his or her clients can help them express their values and visualize their legacy. Coaching helps guide challenging discussions about family members and can bring everyone to the table in the spirit of working together toward a goal, even if the goal is difficult to envision or verbalize. It's not the first skill you'd associate with an attorney, but when you're creating a plan capable of generating an authentic legacy, it's a skill you'll soon come to deeply appreciate.

Don't lock that drawer too tight.

In my experience, once an estate plan is fully implemented, clients often breathe a sigh of relief and move on to tackle the next project that they have procrastinated about for too long. Not so fast! An estate plan is only as good as its most recent update. The fact is, things change. Asset protection laws evolve, tax laws are amended, clients' assets grow or decline, and, most importantly, clients' wishes change as their families mature and expand. An estate plan that is rigid and unchanging is likely obsolete shortly after it is signed.

An estate plan must be viewed as an evolving work that changes as life changes. Estate planning has too often been viewed as a transaction—something to be completed and crossed off the to-do list. Remember when investments were primarily sold by stockbrokers who made commissions based on each transaction? Today, most wealthy families work with financial planners who focus on the relationship with the client rather than creating a volume of transactions. Estate planning clients should demand the same from their legal team—an ongoing relationship that is committed to keeping the clients' estate plan up-to-date permanently.

In the late 1990s, as I was developing my practice, I took a close look at other lawyers' estate planning practices and discovered that most people's plans did not work as they had intended—not because of poor drafting, but because the originally well-drafted plans had never been updated. They had been filed away, never to see the light of day until the client passed away. This is when I decided to start a "formal" updating program—a program with set expectations rather than empty aspirations. My clients pay a modest annual fee, and my staff commits to doing annual tasks intended to identify and correct weaknesses in clients' plans. On our updating program, my clients meet with us face-to-face at least every three years, regardless whether they recognize the need for updates.

The results of participation in the updating program have been substantial. Because my client's plans are kept current, administration of their plans upon disability or death is more efficient, less time consuming, and less expensive—their plans work the way they were intended to work.

Brad Galbraith

THE COMMITMENT

Tax laws and financial regulations are enormously complex. No surprise there. What might surprise you is how fluid they are. These laws and regulations are often updated and revised annually or even more frequently. Staying current is a significant commitment that has real consequences for your plan. Non-compliance can go undetected for years, only to rear an

ugly head when it's time to settle the estate. Look for professionals who have made the commitment to professional designations and who continue to learn with frequent industry
conferences and symposia. Ask if they teach anywhere or if
they have a social media presence. Maybe they even have a
book. . .

FAMILY OFFICES

Ultra-wealthy families have been utilizing so-called "family offices" for years. In fact, many of the strategies and possibilities
you've encountered along the Four Corners were first developed for these super-high-net-worth families. Let's assume your
estate totals somewhere south of the Rockefeller neighborhood,
but that doesn't mean you can't borrow a cup of sugar from
them.

On numerous occasions we've worked with clients who are
assembling their own family office with a dream team of advisors and other professionals who are just right for their family.
It's not unlike being your own general contractor on a home
you build—it requires more than merely approving bathroom
fixtures, but the home you build is often better built and better
suited to your family.

Who's in your virtual family office? The major roles
are your estate planning attorney, your financial advisor/
money manager, your insurance advisor, and CPA. If there's
a business in the mix, make room for the attorney and your
CPA for your business, maybe even your business partners.
For trust-based plans, the trustees may be invited to the table
as well.

Talking Your Way into a Transition

According to various surveys, a majority of estate plans experience some level of post-transition collapse. It is not unusual to see siblings sue one another, resign from trustee positions for fear of being sued, withdraw from family life, or lose their assets. One of the primary reasons for these estate plan failures is that most families are not prepared for the post-transition period. As a result, there is often a breakdown of trust and communication within the family unit. It doesn't help that parents are reluctant to share information about their estate because they fear that it will diminish their children's motivation and distort their values.

In my experience, the way to promote positive communication, build stronger bonds, and avoid having your estate plan come unglued at your death is to hold family meetings. The purpose of family meetings can vary but should always promote meaningful communication, give encouragement, and foster cooperation. It should provide time for decision making, problem solving, and sharing of information and ideas. The meetings can be formal or flexible and informal. In either case, the meetings should encourage each family member to participate.

I encourage my clients to conduct annual family meetings to cover major issues, such as establishing and updating family goals and reviewing the estate plan. If possible, I recommend members of the clients' planning team attend, take notes, and contribute to the discussions when appropriate. Often, I am called upon to review the estate plan we helped put in place, sometimes without the financial details. My experience is that these family meetings almost

(continued)

always turn out to be a synergistic experience for everyone involved.

Family meetings can solve so many problems relating to estate plans. For example, we frequently recommend against leaving assets outright to heirs. By leaving assets in one or more trusts, our clients can protect their heirs. However, a child might think their parents are trying to control them from the grave. This notion is easily dispelled in family meetings, but much harder to deal with after the death of their parents.

The bottom line is that an estate plan will more likely accomplish a client's goals if it is properly explained to the family and the best place for that explanation to take place is in a family meeting with the family's professional advisors present.

Mike Kilbourn

THE MOST IMPORTANT THING YOUR ADVISOR CAN DO

This is a difficult sentence to write: 70 percent of estate plans fail after the primary family members die.

A report in the magazine *Trusts & Estates* reveals that seven out of ten estate plans—plans that were technically well prepared and legally compliant—failed when called on to do what they were designed to do: facilitate the transfer of wealth. The researchers did comprehensive, qualitative interviews with over 3,200 affluent families. They opened the door on deep divisions on the fabric of 70 percent of the post-transition families. From the report:

"Siblings sue one another, resign from trustee positions for fear of being sued, withdraw from family life or lose their assets. In many

families, the only element upon which heirs seem to be able to reach agreement is a willingness to share the cost of hiring a 'will buster.'"

How in the world did things get so bad for so many families? The report points a finger back at the advisors:

"Advisors had so long focused on preparing the assets for heirs and done so effectively. But little was being done to prepare the heirs to receive and manage those assets."

Somebody is not communicating very effectively here and it begins with the advisors.

Advisors are the ones who actually see these failures—they have a broad view and can put each family in context. Clients don't have that view; their knowledge contains only their own experiences. They mean well by trying to keep the details and the dollars secret; they understand the de-motivating power of impending wealth on a young person. They kept them out of the decisions on how the trusts were structured and the assets were to be distributed.

It makes sense on one level: Some of these choices are difficult enough without feeling like one should consult with the heirs named in the trusts. But consulting isn't the point; communication is. After all, it will eventually be their money and their responsibility. Protecting them because they are "not ready" wasn't an option as they were growing into their adult bodies; some things are simply inevitable. Protecting them from their own eventual and inevitable wealth is like trying to protect them from adolescence. It's going to happen, so we better be ready.

WHAT MAKES YOU READY?

Preparing the estate for transition is not as precise as preparing the plan. Every family has its own cultures and codes. Transitioning the family business can sometimes be the catalyst for a more conscious transition and sometimes is at the very center of the black hole. No matter what the situation, there are a few common threads that can be used to light the dark and ease the tension.

We've seen family mission statements that were remarkably successful at capturing the ideas that animate a legacy and a family. Were they well written? Short or long? Aided by a hired advisor or pounded out in private? They were all this and more—and none of it matters.

Family mission statements are not about the statement; they are just documents. What gives them their vitality and their authenticity is the process underneath them. It's about conversation. Candid family dialogues are the raw materials of an enduring legacy. For some, the formality of a family mission statement is just right for starting up the conversational engines. For others, formal structures get in the way. We don't take a strong position on any single approach, but we do—perhaps to the irritation of our more taciturn clients—return again and again to the importance of a dialogue among the family, *about* the family. It's not always convenient or comfortable, but understanding takes time and effort.

In our experiences, the most effective communication sessions don't include dollar amounts, at least not initially. Zeros on a page can quickly take the focus away from what you want to accomplish in the session (and with your plan). And if you have heirs receiving different amounts and different assets at different milestones, look out. A family feud is likely and, unlike the TV game show, this one won't have much hilarity.

Not surprisingly, the best time to prepare for an estate transition is early in your children's and grandchildren's lives. That doesn't mean bringing them to planning meetings when they are too young to count, but it might mean inviting them to participate in small doses as you engage with charitable organizations, even letting them make some decisions on how to distribute charitable contributions. Like all things we master, we started with small wins and worked up.

Earlier we talked about the estate advisor as a coach, and it's tempting to think that client coaching on envisioning a legacy is the same skill that can coach a family toward a successful transition. Our answer: maybe. A coach should have no favorites but the estate advisor as coach may look to the rest of the family as favoring the client more than the rest of the family. If the advisor is perceived as "trying to sell" a plan to the family members, we're already seeing a portion of the room not buying anything. The good news is there are family coaches who specialize in wealth transitions—they don't sell financial products or build estate plans. We've seen these people do wonderful and amazing things with families heading for a transition that initially promised only mistrust and conflict.

Getting Better: Look for Advisors Who Are Committed to Professional Practice

How do you find the right professionals to advise you on the topics and ideas covered in this book? That is an important question when you figure what is at stake—the well-being of your family.

Even if there are numerous professionals in your area to choose from, picking the "right" ones for you and your family may prove to be difficult. Will the ones you select listen to your goals and will they have the knowledge to recommend the best strategy for you and your family? Will they know about how to pass on more than just your wealth and do it in an efficient way with the least amount of court costs, attorney fees, and estate taxes possible?

(continued)

The first step in answering these questions and gaining confidence in your choice is to take time to research the education, experience, and affiliations of the professionals you are considering. Also, look for those who have clearly made a commitment to their profession by going beyond the basic education and certification requirements of their respective field of expertise.

For example, the attorney you select should specialize in estate planning. Then, find out if he or she has taken the next step and become board certified in Wills, Trusts and Estates by their state bar association. It is even better if the attorney you are considering also has a Master of Laws Degree (LL.M.) in taxation or is a Certified Public Accountant (CPA).

When it comes to financial planners and insurance professionals, there is no better way for them to demonstrate their focus and dedication to their profession than by obtaining professional certifications and designations. Start with professionals who have one or more college degrees and then look for designations, such as Chartered Financial Consultant (ChFC), Certified Financial Planner (CFP), Accredited Estate Planner (AEP), Chartered Advisor in Senior Living (CASL), Chartered Advisor in Philanthropy (CAP), etc. It is easy to spot commitment here, as each designation involves a rigorous course of education and testing and only the most committed are willing to do the work.

Beyond all the education and certifications is the professional's involvement in professional associations such as the state bar association, state CPA societies, the Association of Certified Financial Planners, and the Society of Financial Service Professionals.

Even if you find a well educated, focused, and committed individual, he or she must be a good communicator and, above all, be a good listener. Don't hesitate to interview more than one professional and do not feel trapped if, in your initial meeting, they are not able to instill confidence. Be polite, but move on and interview others. It is your legacy; don't entrust its design to anyone but the best.

Mike Kilbourn

PLANTING YOUR TREE

And so we've arrived at the end of the tour—a whirlwind trip through the ideas, insights, opportunities, and questions that come together as the Four Corners Estate Plan. We hope you've learned a few things and maybe unlearned a few more. Evolved estate planning takes the focus away from documents and laws and elevates the dialogue from the conference table surface to real people and real life: you, your spouse, your children and grandchildren, the family you've helped bring forward, and the community you want to lift up.

For readers with a deeper understanding of estate planning and the legal and financial instruments that populate a plan, our aim was to infuse some humanity into the acronyms. For readers new to this particularly odd vocabulary, we wanted to start the conversation on the right foot—with open-ended questions and blue-sky visualization. You *can* do more than you probably imagined, even more than you have ever dreamed.

The word "legacy" is too often seen as big letters engraved atop a building meant to last for generations. Creating things that endure is good work, but only if they are allowed to flex with changing times and generate anew. A legacy isn't a stone; it's a tree. It's planted in the rich soil of your values today, grows across changing seasons, and sends seedlings into the world for germination and new growth. Faith, understanding, and love are what feed this tree. Our work as estate planning professionals is to help you plant your tree where it can thrive and to stand with you and your heirs as they are supported by its strength and nourished by its fruit.

May your legacy grow mightily and may your family prosper year after year.

Staying Current and Going Further

No book on taxes and tax laws stays 100% accurate for long. That's why we created www.fourcornersplan.com. On the website, you'll find updated information on the estate tax, gift taxes, and other tax laws that have evolved since *The Four Corners* was printed. On the website, you'll also discover fresh thinking and insights on some of the strategies that form the Four Corners plan. Finally, you can learn more about the contributing authors, and find links to their individual practices.

The Four Corners is intentionally broad in scope, and not intended to be specific, individual guidance. Before creating an estate plan, or making any estate-related decisions, consult with your financial, tax, and legal advisors.

About Shared Drive Media

Shared Drive Media, LLC helps advisory professionals communicate and helps families succeed in crafting enduring legacies. For more information, visit www.shareddrivemedia.com.